The oldest and strongest emotion of mankind is fear, and the oldest and strongest kind of fear is fear of the unknown.

H.P. Lovecraft

ACKNOWLEDGEMENTS

To my wife Heather, daughter Iris and son Jett, thank you for the love and patience you show me every day. I know I am difficult to live with, but I can cook, mow and fold laundry, and that makes me tolerable.

Thanks to Troy, Lisa, Sandy, Julie, Bobbi and the rest of the American Hauntings Tours family!

Thank you to Chasidy and Len, and anyone else who tagged along on investigations. It's nice not going alone to these places!

Lastly, I would like to thank all of those who allowed me to write about their experiences. It means a lot to me to have people share their stories with me. I can't thank you by your real names, but you know who you are!

CREEPY
WITH A CHANCE OF GHOSTS

LUKE
NALIBORSKI

American Hauntings Ink

ORIGINAL COVER ARTWORK DESIGNED BY

THIS BOOK PUBLISHED BY:

American Hauntings Ink
228 South Mauvaisterre Street
Jacksonville, Illinois | (217) 791-7859
Visit us online at http://www.americanhauntingsink.com

First Edition – August 2017
ISBN: 978-1-892523-03-7

Printed in the United States of America

TABLE OF CONTENTS

INTRODUCTION

Time for another collection of investigations and stories that I acquired through the years. Sometimes the stories are brought to me, and sometimes I have to seek them out. The ones I have gathered inadvertently can be as easy as merely bringing up the idea of ghosts to people. Not everybody is interested in the topic though, so I try to tread softly with this subject. Usually what I will do is toss the ghost bait out there, give it a couple little jiggles as I reel it in, and see if the person bites. If they don't bite, I'll just reel it in and put the topic away. If they nibble, then I'll not only jiggle the bait, but I might zig and/or zag the bait just to entice them. Generally, I can tell within a minute or two if they are interested in the subject so I don't waste either of our time with foolish conversation.

Since I opened up my own vintage toy shop recently, I now have a venue where I can continuously sell my books. Along with the vintage toys, I also carry a lot of horror related toys and ghost literature. This, in turn, has also opened up a lot of opportunities to talk to individuals about their ghost stories whether current or old. Not only that, but I can also sit behind my sales counter, greet customers and write. This is an ideal situation for me because even when the store is not selling stuff, I am writing, which will hopefully bring me sales in the future. Obviously, that has worked because you are reading the book now, so for that I am grateful.

As I began doing some investigations and collecting stories, I began to realize that the new book wasn't too far off, and I started hitting it a little harder to try and finish it off. If you have read my past books, I am sure you'll notice my writing style has not strayed terribly from book to book. I try to stay true to myself and keep my stories interesting and entertaining. If you put the book down mid-story for any reason other than to use the bathroom, then I may not be doing my job as a storyteller. I want you to be engaged in the stories, and I try to make you feel like you are listening to me tell you a story in person.

I am also hopeful that with this new book, my writing skills are improving as well. That being said, I write the way I speak, so my grammar may not be the best. Just bear with it and hang in there. This book isn't supposed to make you feel like you are reading a college textbook. It's supposed to make you laugh and scare you at the same time and hopefully fulfill your wildest fantasies. If there are errors, it's ok. Don't judge me. Treat the errors as if they are adding character to the story.

I usually try to open my books with some little quip from my childhood that ties to ghosts, adventures and other odds and ends. Sadly, my childhood stories have already been conveyed in the last few books. I'm really starting to question how special my childhood actually was. So, as I sit here contemplating on an introduction that will flow seamlessly into the book, I do have a few stories that will hopefully be consistent with what you expect from me. I will do my best to keep them in the lines of the paranormal, or at least abnormal, since that is what you were looking for when you decided to read my book.

I was trying to think of something scary that happened to me in the past couple years that you may enjoy reading about. I wanted to come up with something that was possibly paranormal, to really set the tone for the adventures you are about to go on. Since the story would be part of my intro, it had to be something that would not constitute a full story devoted to it, but rather just a little excerpt to engulf you in the writings to come. I was able to come up with one particular event that happened to me during the fall of 2016. This event scarred me and made me fearful to ever go into a gas station restroom again. Just thinking about putting it down on paper makes me shutter with ....antici....pation. (Have to pay homage to Rocky Horror!)

If any of you ever encounter something like this, do not investigate, run. Run fast, and don't look back. If there are others with you, leave them. Knock them down; rub hot sauce in their eyes, whatever you have to do to save yourself. This story is not for the faint of heart though either. If you recently ate, do not continue reading for about an hour or two so your food can settle. Actually, just to make this more fun, let's turn this story into a "choose your own adventure" kind of tale. So, if you feel you can handle it, that all your years of experience have prepared you for what you are about to read, continue on to the next paragraph. If your first thought was, whoa, slow down, wait a minute, then you can skip ahead about seven paragraphs. The adventure is yours. Choose your fate now.

If you are still with me, you choose wisely. It's best that you hear this story with the hopes that it may possibly prepare you for a similar encounter that you may become part of in the future. If you come across a situation like this, you can think to yourself "WWLD" also known as "What Would Luke Do". Recalling this story may be your only chance of survival if you are thrown into harm's way, as I was. Strap yourself in, this ride is about to get bumpy.

When I head out to Alton to conduct one of the Alton Hauntings Tours, I always stop at a local gas station along the way just so I can get some holy water, aka Mountain Dew. I also use this stop as a means for going to the bathroom prior to the tour. If I don't use the gas station restroom, then I have to possibly use the restroom at the First Unitarian Church (one of our most haunted locations on our tour) prior to the tour starting. By going into the church early, it also means being alone inside the building, which isn't the greatest feeling in the world. When you are going to the bathroom in a haunted location, it's hard to not feel vulnerable. So now you can see why taking care of business at the gas station makes sense. On this bathroom trip, the big, bad scary church would have been like visiting a candy shop compared to the gas station.

When I opened the restroom door and turned the light on, I got the shock of my life. No, it had nothing to do with scattering cockroaches. The bathroom was absolutely, utterly destroyed. The toilet, the walls, the trashcan were all dripping with it. Of course, you are probably thinking I am referring to blood. Or, maybe if it wasn't blood, perhaps it was urine? Trust me, I would have rather it been one of those two substances that spray painted the room. Unfortunately for my virgin eyes, I encountered wall to wall poop.

Whoever did this, was truly a master of his craft. Everything in that bathroom was his canvas and he really explored the space. There was poop on the walls, poop all over the toilet seat, and poop on the floor. It was even on the sink for crying out loud! How is that even possible? I suppose he could have perched on the sink like a bald eagle and did it. Using my detective abilities however, makes me find that impossible. With how much of this stuff was strewn about, he had to have been a pretty large guy which would have made balancing on the sink pretty difficult. Maybe he was acting like a monkey and throwing it with his hands. He was clearly an artist, so perhaps finger painting was one of his mediums.

At this point you are probably thinking this is pretty disgusting, but yet you continue to read. Even after everything I've told you, there was one other detail that I left out that really seals the deal on this terrifying encounter. Along with the feces cascading down the side of the trashcan, the poop bandit also left his calling card inside the trashcan. Nestled softly on top of the pile of paper towels and normal trash, was his "meadow muffin" soaked underwear! At that point, I was concerned that he still was out there, somewhere, armed and dangerous. Even scarier, he was running amok commando. Amok, amok, amok for all you "*Hocus Pocus*" fans. He may even still be in the gas station peering over the potato chip section to see the responses from the victims as they left the bathroom. If he wasn't still in the vicinity, I was hoping he wasn't on his way out to my tour that night.

As if seeing this epic destruction wasn't bad enough, I had to take the walk of shame and inform the sales clerk that someone's butt exploded in the bathroom. I had to hope that she didn't think it was me that did it either. I didn't even use the bathroom during that visit. I knew that whatever I did in that bathroom wouldn't even come close to what the guy did before me, so why even try. I gave him the respect he deserved by acknowledging his work, and then moved on. I grabbed my Mountain Dew, paid the bill, and got in my car.

As I was pulling away, I think I saw one of the employees wearing a HAZMAT suit walking towards the bathroom. It was a somber walk, but one with purpose. The artistic stylings had to be washed away so no other person would experience what I did that night. What a start to a ghost tour. I even informed my crowd prior to the tour that no matter what scary things happened to us during the tour; it would not top what I experienced on the way there. I wish I would have taken a photograph of the crime scene just so you could see the sheer devastation. It was like a shock and awe campaign. War time photography isn't really my thing though, so I didn't think to do it at the time.

For those that skipped ahead to this spot, glad to have you back. You can continue reading without any concerns of losing your lunch from this point on. I do want to say however, that last adventure is a 100% true story. Although I feel I am creative, that's not something I could make up. I would rank that story as paranormal, because trust me; there was nothing normal about the whole situation. We do need to get back on task though with the ghost stories so let's continue.

There are a lot of different stories in the pages to come. I only selected the stories that I felt would contain enough content to include in the book. I did go on a few other investigations that really didn't pan out with collecting actual evidence, which I feel are better left out of the book. They do however make great short stories for the introduction.

One of these stories in particular that I would like to share, involves a gentleman who has had several experiences inside his home. I was debating about writing the story at all, but as he was telling me the story, he was all for me writing it. In fact, I think he was excited about that possibility. So, I'll just put a little of the info out there for you. For the investigation, it was Chasidy, Julie, Sandy and I. When we arrived at the house, the owner met us in front of the house and began to tell us about all these things he encounters. Some of the things he mentioned are very strange and I was getting excited at the possibilities that could lie on the other side of the door.

For the history of the home, a man did take his life inside the home not too long ago. Whether or not this individual is haunting the building is still up in the air. As you will find out as the story goes further, I am not so sure it's the house or the man who committed suicide causing the activity.

After hearing about some of the things he was seeing, it was quickly becoming something I have never experienced before. Some of the images he was describing just didn't make sense. When I asked him how often he sees things, he said every day. At this point I started to really try to get a bit more information out of him as to when and how he sees these things. It turns out he sees these images by items being manipulated. For example, a plastic bag would be formed into an image of an evil face. Sometimes he would see things, other times he would see people, just by looking at an object. He's had to get rid of various household items because he feels that they are getting taken over by the spirits. One such item he disposed of was his clock because it had been possessed. He also had to get rid of one of his cats because it was acting differently and was always hissing at things. Not only was it reacting at something, it also attacked the home owner and caused a huge gash in his leg.

He even admits that some of the things that he has seen seem very far-fetched. He has a hard time believing what he has been seeing but he has no doubts that they are there. He's seen pharaohs, dictators, angels, Jesus, a baggy breasted hag, one horned dinosaurs and lightning. Sometimes he sees the spirits face with his mouth open trying to look ferocious. These are just some of the visions he's had. All of these things he has seen during his stay inside this home. It doesn't follow him to other places he goes to. These things also didn't start to occur until he moved into this home less than fifteen years ago.

When we went inside, we began setting up some equipment to try and gather some evidence. He had another paranormal team there before which he said documented some great activity, so we were hopeful. While in the house he pointed out a blanket that had just been manipulated recently. To him it looked like three claw marks had run across the blanket. To me, it just looked like wrinkles, but I could see what was making him think the way he did. It may just be an overactive imagination, or it could be something more. He has had some physical abuse from the spirit as well. He has been assaulted with punches to the ribs as well as being choked. So, things like that may or may not be things that his imagination could create. Especially if there are visible marks leftover from these attacks.

After investigating for about an hour, we decided to go a different route with what we were doing. None of us had any heebie jeebies feelings when we came into the house, so it didn't have a bad vibe to it; well at least it didn't that night. All of us really felt like anything that may be going on in the house seemed to be centered on him. He was the one seeing everything, his wife didn't see any of it, and we didn't see any of it. Since it was all tied to him and how his mind worked, I didn't feel that we were going to be able to capture any evidence other than his stories. I felt that a lot of what was going on had to do with the way his mind worked. Perhaps his mind was just operating at a different level than ours and it was causing him to study things with a lot more detail than the rest of us.

Due to what he was experiencing and his hope that it would go away, we did do a cleansing of him. I wasn't sure if that would help him or not, but we definitely didn't feel like it would do him any harm either. We also gave him some advice for the future when these types of things happened. Perhaps if he didn't try to look too hard at things to try and see something that's not there, he wouldn't find a need to do it any longer. It's like those "Magic Eye" posters. When you look through something, or past it, sometimes you see something that isn't there. I think that's what he may have been doing.

As far as what our investigating turned up, there were a few things of note. When we first got in there, I had my Ghost Radar running. I asked if there was anyone with us right now and the word "author" came up. Although debatable, I guess I am an author and I was there. So, I found that interesting and a little flattering. As we began setting up equipment, Sandy placed her Rem-Pod on a pile of items that were covered with a blanket. The pod started to go off almost immediately. This seemed like very odd behavior for the gadget. Usually it only goes off zero to two times per investigation, but this was going off every few seconds. Sandy said there were new batteries in it, so we knew that power loss wasn't causing the issue. We then started to look around the area and we ended up finding a power cord running underneath the pile of clutter. We traced the cord and it led to a surge protector with about three or four things plugged into it. Nothing paranormal causing the reaction from the Rem-Pod, just a major fire hazard.

There was a point in the investigation where we were inside and then we went outside for a bit. When we came back in to retrieve some equipment, I noticed the light was turned on in the room we were focusing on. I knew the light was out when we walked out of the house because I had checked my camera to make sure the infrared was working properly. When I reviewed the video later, it turned out the owner had come back into the house for something and he turned the light on. He left the room without turning the light back off. I definitely don't think he did it on purpose to contaminate the evidence, he just forgot to turn it off. It was a letdown though unfortunately. I was hoping that it could have been a piece of evidence for the investigation. At no other point on the video or the audio did I get anything worthy of presenting as paranormal evidence.

This investigation shows that sometimes the activity seems to be in one person's mind. That makes it very difficult to conduct an investigation because we can't look into that individual's mind. We can only look at tangible evidence that we can capture to show others. Hopefully after our visit, he didn't put himself into situations to allow his mind to work that way. Again, I can't say for sure the house isn't haunted, but I don't think it is.

This is just one example of an investigation that I've done recently where the outcome didn't lend itself to writing about it. Even then, the story was interesting and a bit strange. One other thing of note that I've encountered over the past couple years baffles me. I speak every year at the Espenschied Chapel in Mascoutah, IL. I have also put on a ghost event there a couple times during the spring. For some reason, I've had numerous people tell me that they have seen a bluish glow around me as well as a bluish shape behind me when I am on stage speaking. I am assuming that the glow around me must be my aura. I've talked to a few people about it and they were all quick to say that it's just my aura and nothing to be worried about. When I looked into this a bit more, I found something interesting. Would you believe that having a blue aura represents creativeness and intelligence? Also, people with blue auras are good at writing?? Well, at least they got the creative part right. Not so much with the intelligence and being a good writer. Well maybe I am a good writer too. After all, I was able to turn a poop story into sheer poetry just a little while ago.

As far as the blue shape that was standing behind me, I am not really sure what that represents. I have been to a lot of haunted locations, so hopefully nothing is attached to me. If you have read my earlier works, I mentioned the possibility of me having a guardian angel that has been around during times of need. Maybe that shape is my angel. I don't really know for sure, but I know it's not threatening, so I am good with it.

The intro is turning into a lot longer story than I thought, so I feel it best we get to the actual ghost stories I intended for this book. We are going to hit a lot of different locations and most of these have never been written about before. We'll visit several private residences, a library, a former hotel and even a courthouse! Most of the locations I have had the honor of investigating and the remaining stories were ones that were told to me by people who experienced the hauntings themselves!

With this book, I am bringing back what I did for my last book "*Ghosts Never Say Boo!*" and am adding audio files to my website **www.ghostsneversayboo.com**. Basically, by doing this, it makes the book interactive for you. You don't have to take my word for what we heard at an investigation, you can listen to it for yourself. I didn't put all the audio up, but for the files that are there, it'll tell you what page in the book the audio is from. I found this to be a great tool to really make you feel like you are a part of the investigation. In some cases, the audio may not be as clear as when we heard it and in other cases, you may hear something completely different and that's ok. All evidence could be interpreted differently. If everyone agreed that it's all ghostly, then we wouldn't have to search for answers anymore and where's the fun in that. What I do is put the stories out there, give you the evidence we acquired and then you can take it from there.

Another fun thing with this book is I collaborated on a story with Brian Gray. Brian hosted the Ste. Genevieve Ghost Tours for the past few years. I asked

Brian if there was a story that I could interview him about for the book and he one upped me by actually writing the story. I went in and cleaned up some things and of course had to add to it a bit. Hopefully you enjoy this little addition to the book. Brian writes a lot like I do so it should flow quite well.

I also want to apologize if I explain how equipment works a few times throughout the book. When I write my stories, I write them as I experience them. Often times I have the same thoughts from investigation to investigation and I convey those thoughts through my writing. Instead of thinking about my writing as an epic story, just think of it as a collection of themes or short stories of which there may be repetition in my thought process.

The idea behind this book's title is that not all locations that look creepy are haunted and not all picture-perfect houses are innocent. There are some spots that we go to that by looking at the front of the building; you just know that it has to be haunted. Then there are others that look very peaceful and serene and when you walk through the doors, things are being thrown at you by unseen hands. You just can't judge a book by its cover, nor a haunted house. With that in mind and without further ado, I bring you the latest in my writings, "*Creepy with a Chance of Ghosts*"!

THE GIRL ON THE STAIRS

My dear friend Mary passed on another possible investigation to me in late 2015. Although the timing was bad for me at the moment, it was definitely one that I was looking forward to getting around to doing. 2016 brought an opportunity for me to finally have some free time that I could devote to this wonderful hobby of mine.

I reached out to Missy early 2016. After trading some texts back and forth, a date was set up for me to come out and visit the home. Much like other investigations I have conducted, this was going to start off with an initial interview of Missy. I like to start off this way, so I can get a feel for the homeowner. It's also a chance to try to write off things naturally if possible. You can weed out lots of activity within that first visit; which in turn will save you some time later on if the location doesn't warrant bringing out all of your equipment as well as team members.

For this opening interview, I prefer to only bring the basics. The arsenal will include my digital recorder for recording the stories as they are told to me by the person who experienced them. I have found this to be an incredible tool to help recall not only the stories later, but it also helps to capture the emotion in the person's voice when they are telling the stories. Writing them down in a notebook does not always capture the true fear, or enjoyment, behind the story. I also brought my digital camera, so I could photograph some of the areas that seem to be the most active. Lastly, and most importantly, I brought my friend Chasidy with me. Chasidy not only is a valuable asset to the story collection and investigating, it is also nice to have someone along for safety. Do not judge Chasidy by her size; she can be a little firecracker.

The home was built in 1902 in a small farming community down in southern Illinois. It is a two-story house with an addition of a kitchen area and bathroom built on the backside of the home. There's a small shed in the back that is also original to the home, but it does not play into the story. Although located on the "wrong side of the tracks", the neighborhood seemed to be fine. The bad area is actually a couple blocks to the west. Although the street was dark which made it difficult to see the house numbers, we eventually did locate the home. I have always made it a habit to look at the location via online maps so I can see what the house looks like. This not only helps me get pepped up to do an investigation if the house looks really creepy, it also helps in locating the house if the conditions are not conducive to seeing house numbers.

This particular home was purchased by Missy in 2013. It was a foreclosure and right out the gate, Missy was seeing how considerate the former tenants were. While going through the kitchen cabinets, she found several love notes left for her. Most said something to the extent of "You are going to die in this house". It also appeared that whoever lived there before, most likely upon finding out that they were losing the home, decided to break tons of glass bottles in the backyard. This was assumed as the yard was littered with broken glass. She is constantly picking up glass so her grandchildren can play in the yard without slicing their feet open.

She has done a lot of work to the inside of the home as well. The previous owners must have had several big dogs. Most of the carpets were stained beyond repair, so all of it had to be completely torn up. Upon doing that, original hardwood floors were found below. Quite possibly the renovations that Missy has done may be what is causing the activity to occur.

Missy met us at the door and brought us into the front room first. It is a little living area with a television, couch and chairs. Since that room doesn't have any heat leading to it and she does not typically spend much time in there, she sectioned it off by hanging a blanket in the doorway that leads to another family room. The difference in temperature between these two rooms was crazy. It was nothing paranormal though, just a skillful way to moderate what is getting heated and what is not. We sat down on the couch in this family room, and I immediately began to give Missy a history of what I am about. After a few hours of talking about me, I finally decided to give Missy a chance to talk. Of course, I am kidding about the length of time I spoke about myself, but I do think it makes the homeowner feel more comfortable if they know a little bit about the person they are bringing into their home. I usually just mention how long I have been doing paranormal investigations and what my intentions are with the investigation. I also try to name drop Troy Taylor when I can since he has some street cred in the field. After boring her with my life history, it was time to start to gather the stories from the home. The following is a rundown of what she has experienced in the two years she has lived in this home.

When Missy first bought the house, she didn't sense anything strange. She does come from a family that tends to have an ability to pick up on things though. Whether it is feeling a disturbance in the energy of an area, or having dreams that in some cases do come true, several members of her family possess this skill. The dream aspect always creeps me out. I definitely agreed with Missy when she said she always made it clear to her mom that if a dream was about something bad happening to her, she didn't want to know. Especially since some of the dreams were about people dying.

The initial tenants under Missy's ownership were herself, her daughter and her daughter's two young children. The house was purchased just before Thanksgiving, and the family was excited that they would be able to celebrate the holiday at the new home. The celebration was centered in the family room that we were doing the initial interview. Although a make shift table was set up in the center of the room, there were a lot of unpacked boxes and tubs scattered all about the room so space was at a premium.

It was during this holiday that Missy witnessed her first paranormal experience at the home. If you come out of the kitchen area, you will find yourself in the dining room. Once you come out of the kitchen and into dining room, to the left is the staircase that leads upstairs. To the right is the doorway that leads into the family room. Missy came out of the kitchen and

The little girl would be seen peering between the two spindles at the bottom of the stairs.

out of the corner of her left eye, she saw a little girl sitting on the bottom few steps of the staircase. Of course, upon doing a double take, the little girl was gone.

According to Missy, this was not the only time that she saw the little girl. The girl tends to frequent the bottom of the stairs. She likes to look between the stairwell spindles with her hands holding two spindles and her face gazing out in between them. Picture Jack Nicholson in *The Shining* as he's peering through the broken door to totally get the image. Maybe even give him long hair to make it more realistic for you.

Missy's daughter also encountered this little girl in a bit of a different way. Several times when she would be walking up the stairs or down the stairs, she would feel the need to get over to one side of the staircase. It was a feeling as if something else was coming down or going up and to be considerate, you move to one side. Although nothing was seen, that was the feeling that she got. Even though it wasn't visible, she got the sensation that it was a little girl that made her hug the wall and she scampered up and down the steps every time a situation like this came about.

Although visitors usually they see the little girl on the staircase or feel her move past them, that's not the only way they encounter her. Other times the child is experienced by a cold spot on the staircase. There is a window by the steps, so that could be the cause of the cold areas they have felt. The argument against that being the source is it does occur at all times, even when it is warm out.

As I was being told these stories, I decided to resituate myself on the couch. I moved further down to a spot where I could see right into the dining room. This gave me a perfect view of the bottom of the staircase. Prior to changing locations, I got a sharp pain in my hand and I felt a burning sensation like I had been scratched.

When I looked at my hand I did indeed get scratched. I didn't realize Missy's cat was still by me and when I moved, it must have got startled and scratched me. I had been petting the cat most of the time we were on the couch, but it slipped my mind that I still was when I got up to move.

One day, Missy was shopping when she received a phone call from her very frantic daughter. At first Missy thought that maybe her daughter's ex, the kids' dad, was bothering them and that was why she was so distressed. While Missy was talking to her about who she needed to call to take care of the situation, her daughter began to tell her to stop talking because she didn't understand. She was freaking out because she saw her daughter sitting on the bottom of the staircase, so she started to yell at her to get to bed. Since all her daughter would do is stare at her and not listen, the yelling got louder and Missy's daughter watched as this little girl disappeared right in front of her. The actual daughter was later found already in her bedroom asleep. The little girl looked so much like Missy's granddaughter that a mistake had been made.

Missy spoke of another time where she was vacuuming the upstairs hallway. She saw her granddaughter move past her into one of the bedrooms, so she began to talk to her. Seconds later her granddaughter called to her mom from the kitchen. Missy looked in the bedroom where she saw the girl go, but there was no one there.

The girl has been encountered quite often and has been consistent with the descriptions people give after seeing her. She is seen wearing a light maroon colored dress. She has dark hair and light-colored eyes. Her hair is pulled back and tied with a light-colored ribbon. Her image is incredibly detailed by Missy, which to me, means that she has more than just fleeting glimpses of this ghost. Most of you probably realize, this is not very common in the least.

Missy also mentioned that she got involved with a Facebook group that was for a psychic community. Missy had commented on someone's post, and after that, she received a message from someone who lived in Las Vegas. Keep in mind, Missy never told anyone in this Facebook group about what she had going on in her home. This person told Missy that she had a message for her from the little girl on her stairs. This girl wanted Missy to know that when the little girl isn't there, the older ladies are. The little girl also told the psychic to tell Missy that she was related to her. The girl's name is Carolyn, and she had a sister named Marilyn.

This caught Missy off guard for several reasons. First, Missy has a lot of half siblings. Her father had been married several times and had multiple sets of children with each wife. Two of these children were twin sisters. One of them, Marilyn, lived to be old, but Carolyn, died when she was five years old. This happened twenty years before Missy was born. The second interesting thing out of this is Missy didn't talk about this with people. Only a few people even knew about how much family she had because of her father's marriages. Lastly, the idea of this girl ghost being related to her, could explain why she looks so much like her granddaughter. Missy doesn't really know who the older ladies are that inhabit the home. Perhaps they were in the house long before Missy even got there.

She thought maybe one of the older women ghosts could have been her mom. She had passed away years before so it was possible. Missy did experience her mother a couple times after she passed away, but that was in another home. Two different times her music box started playing on its own. The first time it started playing was when Missy was thinking about her mom. It played for about 6 seconds. After it stopped, Missy picked the box and up and started to shake it to see if would play again, but it didn't. The crazy thing is that the music box has to be wound in order to play, and the key that was used to do that, had been lost years prior. So, for several years, the music box sat dormant. The second time it went off was on her mom's birthday.

When Missy first began remodeling her house, a lot of stuff was put into tubs to store. She mentioned that she had bought three brand new smoke detector sets and they were put into one of the tubs. When she went to get them so they could be installed, they also somehow vanished. To this day she has yet to find out what had happened to them. Also during renovations, tools and other fixtures were disappearing. Perhaps this was the spirits way of telling Missy they didn't like what she was doing to the house.

When Missy would do laundry in the basement, clean clothes would usually be put into a laundry basket until she would have a chance to put them away. Several times she would find clothes hung up in her closet that didn't belong there. These would be items that Missy would always put in her dresser or in various other places. They would not have been put there by her, so my initial thought was that the ghosts must be helpful ones and are helping her with the household chores.

In the kitchen area, sometimes the cabinets would be opened up on their own. Side note, I wonder why this happens a lot in haunted homes. It seems like this is one of the most common ways for spirits to get the attention of the families, so maybe that's why they do it. Well that and I would have to think it gets very annoying to have to keep constantly shutting them. This is something that if I were a ghost, I would find great enjoyment in doing.

She also mentioned that sometimes ice will get thrown across the room from the refrigerator. In my mind, I was picturing the evil apple trees in *The Wizard of Oz*, but in this case instead of an apple hurling tree, I was seeing an ice hurling fridge. Those visions were quickly washed away by the thought of an ice cube being stuck in the ice dispenser area. Then the ice would slowly melt, until it fell through the slot and then would hit the ground. Then, not to go into too much physics, due to momentum and lack of friction, the ice would slide across the floor to the other side of the kitchen. Before I could mention this idea, Missy suggested the same idea. That was one of the great things about her stories; she was trying to explain things naturally all the time. Not everything was 100% paranormal in her mind.

Missy said that the spirits hate being ignored in her house. If they wanted to get her attention, one of the most common things they would do is to knock on the walls. If Missy doesn't acknowledge the sound, the knocks will keep getting louder and louder until she finally tells them to knock it off. Then the knocking will stop and the spirits will be happy that they got what they wanted. The knocking seems to be coming from where her bedroom is, but if she's in her bedroom, she never hears it.

Sometimes when Missy is on the first floor she will hear the sound of someone walking on the second floor. It usually sounds like heavy boots walking in the rooms, back and forth in the hallway, and up and down the stairs. She even heard these footsteps earlier in the day that we came out for the interview.

During renovations, after she got the home insulated, she and the inspector had just come down to the first floor and were standing at the bottom of the stairs. They were talking when all of a sudden, the sound of someone walking upstairs made the inspector turn and look up the stairs. He turned back to Missy and asked if she heard that. Missy asked him what he heard and he of course mentioned that it sounded like someone was up there. They both knew that area was empty because they were just in that area of the house.

Missy's bedroom closet seems to be very active as well. Aside from the laundry being hung up in her closet for her, she also hears mumbling late at night. Often times when she is lying in bed trying to go to sleep, she will hear what sounds like a conversation between two women, coming from the closet. We all know how annoying two women talking in a closet can be....am I right guys? Fist bump! Missy would then turn the television on just to cover the sound of the gossiping women.

One night, Missy's daughter was having issues with her dude, so she decided to bring the kids and herself to Missy's to stay the night. Her daughter had to leave early in the morning, so she knocked on the door to Missy's room to let her know the kids were still going to be there. She heard the lamp turn on and saw the light come from under the door, but there wasn't a peep out of Missy. So, her daughter opened the door and peered in. Although the light was turned on, Missy was still fast asleep. When awakened and questioned, she did not turn the light on. Someone, or maybe something, must have done it for her.

One of the other bedrooms on the second floor also has an active closet; this one doesn't have two women yapping away, it has two guys talking about sports. Just kidding of course, but it does have activity. The most common thing that happens in that closet is the light has a mind of its own. It will turn off and on with no explanation as to why.

Missy's phone was also given a little attention by the spirits. Strange messages would appear on her phone with no source. Sometimes the phone would send out random, often times misspelled, messages to people late at night. She took the phone to her carrier and explained what was happening but they assured her that that was not possible.

After talking with some of the neighbors about the home, Missy found that several people experienced very similar things. They all spoke about the voices and the sounds of people walking about. Perfectly meshing with the story though, nobody spoke of ever seeing the little girl. Since I feel that spirit is tied to Missy, it would only make sense that she wouldn't have been experienced prior to Missy purchasing the home.

One Sunday during the summer, Missy was sitting on her couch watching television. She had her laptop next to her and was looking at it, and then she would look back at the television. All of a sudden, she looked up towards the wall and she saw a shadow person walking right past her. She knew right away it was her deceased dad. Years ago, he was involved in a serious car accident. He broke his hip as well as his back. Because of this accident, he walked very oddly. According to Missy, the shadow figure she saw had the same exact gate that her father had. She immediately called her sister and told her about it. Her sister said that he had visited her a couple times as well. She would often experience her dad sitting on her bed. Her son was getting so scared from his visits that she finally told him not to come around anymore, and he hasn't.

Missy's daughter and grandchildren eventually moved back into the home. The kids were unfortunately having a tough time falling asleep in the spare bedroom. They constantly spoke of seeing something peering in at them through the door. The youngest grandchild was terrified. She hated sleeping in that room and would scream until she was rescued by her mom or grandma.

Missy's daughter had an experience of her own during this return to the house. Missy had left in the evening to run to a friend's house. She returned very late at night and went straight to bed. The next morning her daughter mentioned that the night before she heard someone come in the front door and then she heard them in the kitchen, opening the fridge door. Upon going down to see who it was, she found the room to be empty. Missy's daughter and children moved out shortly after that event.

Missy's friend John has had a couple experiences, but nothing major. Missy feels his house may be haunted though as well. He inherited it from his grandma, and she may be the one that's there. She told me about a couple instances with the house that involved her. Most things happen when they get into a fight. During the day, they had been in a heated argument, so they both went their separate ways. Later that evening, Missy walked down to his house. After knocking for a while, the door finally opened. Missy began to lay into him for taking so long to open the door because it was six degrees out. He had a blank look and when she asked what was wrong, he told her that the air hockey table he bought his kids for Christmas had turned itself on. Not a big deal, until he mentioned that it was unplugged. Missy also told me that sometimes when she would be at his house, she could smell pork chops cooking. John smells this a lot because it's one of the things his grandma loved to make. Another cool thing is she has seen his grandma moving about. She describes it as being similar to seeing heat vapors coming off a road or a car. It looks like a shimmering shape moving about.

Other little things that happened are as follows. Her cat tends to get a bit jumpy around things. It'll look towards the wall, see something, jump and run away.

Photo of the small door at the end of the hall.

The cat actually gets its own bedroom too. It's a creepy room that is actually thought of as the attic. It's unfinished, which may lead to the creepiness of it. Personally, I think the fact that it has a full-size door, that's quite a bit smaller than all the other doors, definitely adds to the creepy level.

Sometimes the television turns itself off and on. If she does actually get to watch the television and she becomes engrossed in a show, a banging noise will start to happen in the kitchen. Missy will finally tell it to knock it off, or if it wants to make some racket, it could wash the dishes to make more noise.

Since it seemed like there was a lot going on, I was feeling that we would have a good chance of experiencing something. One of the things I like to find out though is if there is any kind of pattern to the activity. According to Missy, the mumbling in the closet happens a lot. It's usually late at night or early in the morning. The sound of footsteps is frequent, but she is so used to it, she tends to tune it out. The little girl was seen a lot at first. She seems to see her when there are a lot of people in the house. Family events, holidays, etc. are what typically brings her out.

During that initial visit, we didn't do a whole lot of investigating. We took some photos and some EMF readings, but that was it. We wanted to come back another day and do a full investigation, so that was what we did. A month or so later Chasidy and I returned to the home and this time, we were going to see if we could capture any ghostly phenomenon.

Missy stayed outside the house on her front porch the entire time we were there. This was great as we knew that any noises not caused by the two of us, could potentially be paranormal in nature. First thing I wanted to do was to set up my video camera and have it aiming at the stairs. We already knew the ghostly girl has been seen on the steps, so there was that. I was hopeful that there would be all sorts of activity there because I am a firm believer in staircases being the most haunted location in active homes.

After setting the video camera up, Chasidy and I went upstairs to the closet where Missy would hear the voices. We sat on the floor outside of the closet and began to do an EVP session. We used a digital recorder and the Ghost Radar for this process. We did periodically also use the Ghost Radio, but not too much.

A few minutes into the session we did have a bit of a conversation through the Radar. I always try to be careful not to stretch things to make the words that are communicated to us through the radar make sense. If you are doing that, the findings may not be too accurate. Even though I try not to do this, sometimes it happens. Here is the conversation I was having. This audio is available on my website **www.ghostsneversayboo.com.**

Radar: Carlos
Luke: Is your name Carlos?
Radar: Other
Chasidy: Other
Luke: So, it's a different name?
Radar: A word was mentioned here, but I don't recall what it was. It sounds like "strike" in the audio clip. In the background, you hear me whisper "I'm getting goosebumps like crazy right now."
Radar: Hello
Luke: Hello. Are you communicating with us right now?
Radar: Affect
Luke: (whispers "affect") Are you affecting us? Is that why I am cold right now and getting goosebumps? Is that You?
Radar: Cold
Chasidy: Cold
Radar: Run
Luke: Run. Are you saying we should run?
Radar: Compass
Luke: Which direction?
Radar: Door
Luke: It's pretty active right now.
Chasidy: Yeah

All of this evidence was obviously experienced real time. We of course were able to communicate with something and carry on a conversation. It is so much better to do it this way rather than wait until you get home to review the audio. When you can do it as it happens, it makes you be able to actually react to what's being said. When you review it later, you don't have that option.

When I played the audio back at home to review it, looking for other noises that were captured but not heard at the time, I did pick up something during this same segment. About six minutes after this conversation ended, we picked up something that fit very well into what we were doing.

One good thing I actually learned from paranormal television shows is the use of knocking patterns. Some investigators will knock a pattern on the wall with the hopes that it would be completed by something or someone else. I used this technique with some pretty interesting results. During the audio clip, you will hear me say that I am going to try the pattern again. I do the knock, leaving off the last two notes. There's a pause, and then you hear me say something to the extent of asking if they were able to do it and if they did, we didn't hear it. Shortly after that comment, you hear the two knocks to finish off the pattern.

We took a brief intermission from the EVP session after doing the call and answer segment of our show. During this break, we of course did hear something with our own ears. We heard a male voice saying something from downstairs. I was the only male in the house and I knew it wasn't me. Of course, when this happened, we didn't have any recorders going.

We then started back up again. Several times we got the name "Don" on our ghost radar. Although not sure of the significance, Missy's dad's name was Donald.

So maybe it was something with him being there or someone else from the other side trying to convey a message from him. During that EVP interrogation, several times I was feeling a weird tingling sensation with my hair. Perhaps it was nothing, but it was a bit strange.

After listening to the digital recorder from that part of our evening, I did capture a few other things that seemed strange. Most of this questioning occurred with the Ghost Radio. This segment was about 15 minutes in length. About 13 minutes into it, I had what appears to be a woman whispering. I had the ghost radio in an AM setting which I don't typically use, so I was really excited to have something. I can't quite tell what she's saying, although I did listen to it several times. I think I am going to leave it up to you to decide.

About 20 seconds later, there's another clip where you can hear the same voice. This time I really think the spirit says "He's Coming Back." She sounds very upset and scared. At this point, not thinking I had much with AM, I switched over to FM. Shortly after switching it over, I captured another voice. It's a male voice and was about one minute after the female voice said "he's coming back." The other neat thing with this voice is that it's stretched out over several stations. So, it wasn't a DJ's voice that I picked up. With the speed of the radio scan, when you capture a drawn-out voice, you have to wonder. Unfortunately, with this audio, you have to be the judge.

After this, the activity really slowed down. We had some K2 hits, but not a whole lot. I was trying to get the spirits to reach certain lights for me on the K2, and although it did reach them, it didn't seem like it was in reaction to me asking for it.

I've been a longtime advocate of the Ghost Radar. I use it a lot on my investigations; I've highlighted it during some of my presentations and have just really enjoyed its use. An interesting thing occurred with it during this investigation. At first, I was using my Ghost Radar, but after a while, my phone went dead so I couldn't use it any more. Luckily, we were able to use Chasidy's. The name Carlos appeared on her radar as well as mine. I found that to be interesting. She also received the name Don on

Photo of the staircase taken from the 2nd floor of the house

name Don on hers as well. So, seeing the same name on two different devices intrigued me. I am still doing a lot of fieldwork with this device, but I am really happy with what I've seen so far.

As far as the video I recorded that night, I came up empty. I shot about 2 hours of footage on the staircase, and oddly enough the only time I captured orbs, were when we trounced up and down the steps. I will leave it to you to do the math on what those "orbs" probably were.

That about wrapped up our investigation. She is still having activity come through especially since she started to rehab her kitchen. I was very pleased with what we captured and would love to go back some day. I'd like to try and speak with the little girl or at the very least capture video or an image of her. I don't feel any of the spirits here are scary, and Missy feels the same way. It's a lot easier to coexist with those kinds of ghosts rather than the ones who want to push you down the stairs or pull you out of bed.

THE SMELL OF INCENSE

I think sometimes when there's a ghost haunting a specific area, people quickly jump to conclusions and tag the spirit as an evil presence.

Of course, as a paranormal investigator, I have to say that this is furthest from the truth. I have come across countless stories of spirits being the exact opposite of evil. Although in some cases, the spirits tend to be up to mischief and no good in their attempts to get a person's attention, it doesn't mean they are always little trouble makers. To label them as demonic is quite absurd to me. I am not going to say that spirits can't be angry. If we think of ghosts as being the remaining energy of someone who has passed, don't you think the energy would be the same as when the person was alive? So, if they were angry in life, they'll be angry in death. If they were a jokester in life, it would be the same in death.

The movies and television have done their toll on how spirits are supposed to look. They are supposed to be creepy, with blood covered bodies, sharp teeth and whatever else the makeup artists wanted to use to scare us to death. Of all the ghosts, I have encountered in my 15 years of investigating, I have never once seen a disfigured ghost. Not one time have I been chased down by a ghost with dastardly intentions of harming me in obscene and painful ways. Never have I walked past a mirror only to see my reflection doing different things than I was at that moment. I could go on and on as I have seen my share of horror films. This is what television has accomplished by putting the fear of ghosts and what they can do to a person into the minds of individuals who do not have the honor of investigating haunted locations. The experiences that Jennifer's family has had through the years are in no way what Hollywood would lead one to believe.

I came across a family with a ghost that is in no way malevolent or causing trouble. When this spirit is around, the family doesn't take off running, ending up in the nearest hotel, with whatever they could grab so they can change their soiled pants. This family doesn't get scared at all because their spirit is family, and they know this to be true.

It all started a few years ago when a young lady named Jennifer lost her father. They were very close throughout their entire life together, and he was always there for her. Although the loss was hard, Jennifer always felt him around her in spirit even though he was no longer there in the flesh.

One of Jennifer's first encounters with her father's spirit occurred during a very traumatic time for the family. Although many attempts were made to start a family, they weren't having very much luck. That is until one day when Jennifer informed her husband that she was pregnant. Unfortunately, she would later suffer a miscarriage, and the unborn child was going to have to be removed via surgery. When that terrible day finally came for the surgery, Jennifer was laying in the hospital bed, terrified, sad, dealing with a ton of difficult emotions. I could only imagine what a mother would be going through at a time like that. Sadly, Jennifer was also alone in the room at the time. Well, at least she thought she was alone.

From out of nowhere Jennifer began to smell the aroma of incense burning all throughout the room. Of course, in a hospital, there wasn't any smell other than the typical hospital smell. The incense smell completely engulfed her and Jennifer knew right away that her dad was there. The smell was exactly the same as the day her father was laid to rest. At the Catholic funeral, incense was burned. Now, here in her hospital room, the smell was once again flooding her senses.

Jennifer called out to her dad, and he responded to her clear as day. It was like two people having a conversation in a quiet room. She could hear him perfectly and it reminded her of times where he would be sitting on her bed when she was a little girl, comforting her after a bad dream. He was comforting her this time too, only it wasn't a bad dream. This was reality and Jennifer was going through something very scary, and he was there to make sure she knew that everything was going to be fine.

Because of this conversation, all negativity left her body. Jennifer knew that everything was going to go as planned. Her father was going to be there for her not only through the surgery, but through the rest of her life as well. This wasn't the only time they experienced him either. He makes regular visits to their home and always makes himself known by any means possible. Whether she was in a moment of need, or just needed to be comforted, her father was always there for her even when others weren't.

This smell of incense was something that the family encountered quite often after the father's death. In fact, a mere, couple days after the funeral, Jennifer and her husband Brian, could smell the incense at her mother's house. Later in their own house, when Brian awoke from his slumber to use the potty, he could smell the incense burning all the way down the hallway of their house.

One other incident of note that occurred at the mother's house happened one day when Brian was there by himself. He was at the home doing some work late one evening. As he was working, he got this overwhelming feeling that he shouldn't be there. It was an odd feeling and something he had never experienced there before because he was always welcome in this house. He didn't see anything around him, and he knew that he was alone. As far as what it was that was causing this feeling, he didn't have any idea. After trying to work through this feeling of dread, Brian finally decided it was time to leave. As he gathered his belongings and headed toward the door he got a sensation of a heaviness actually pushing him out the door. Brian is a big dude and for him to have a feeling of someone physically moving him was something he wasn't used to. The daunting feeling didn't actually go away until he was in his truck and he was half way down the long, country driveway. Brian just felt that since it was so late at night, the spirit was tired and wasn't able to sleep with all the noise Brian was making. He knew if he came back in the morning, the feeling would be different.

Quite some time after suffering the earlier miscarriage, Jennifer awoke one night and saw a ball of light moving about their bedroom. The light slowly floated down to the foot of the bed and then it began to change shape. As Jennifer looked at the ball of light, it began to pulsate, emanating all kinds of light around the room. It also seemed to be trying very hard to take the shape of something. After watching the light for what seemed like an eternity, the light was able to project itself into the shape of a young boy. To Jennifer, he appeared to be about ten or maybe eleven years old. She only was him from the waste up because his lower half was being hidden by the footboard of the bed.

His attire made it difficult to distinguish what decade he was from. He just wore a common, solid color t-shirt. Sometimes you can figure out the age a spirit is from by their hairstyle as well, but his hair was nothing special either. This young boy stared at Jennifer for a bit and then slowly turned back into the ball of light. After hovering near the bed for a few seconds in the light form, it began to move up towards the ceiling and then disappeared from view. To this day, she has no idea who this was or why he visited her. Although the whole experience was a little unnerving, it didn't scare her in the least.

Lights like these are seen quite often in the home. This previous instance was the only time one took on the shape of something other than a ball of light. Generally, these balls of light would just float around the bedroom with no sense of intelligence. Their size would be that of a basketball, sometimes maybe a bit smaller. They would be seen in areas of the house where they couldn't be naturally explained by passing headlights.

The family seems to think that their dad plays with the radio a lot. Several times the radio will turn itself on and off again. Jennifer was home alone one day when this phenomenon occurred. She had finally had enough with this activity and she called out to her dad about it. She said, "Dad, if it's you, please stop it. It's scaring me." Ever since she addressed the situation with her father, the radio activity has ceased. They still use the radio that was manipulated too, so it couldn't have been a technical issue with it or I am sure it would still be happening.

Although Jennifer experiences most of the activity, Brian did have a couple other experiences around their home that he shared with me. They live out in the country and one night, Brian was standing outside the home near his driveway. To the south of their home is a small little field. As Brian was looking towards the field, he saw this odd shape start to develop. It was a white misty color and was in the shape of a human. It was walking along the edge of the field and Brian's yard. This shape was only about a hundred feet away, so he was able to see it quite clearly. He could even make out the strides as the ghostly figure moved across his property. After watching it walk along most of the south edge of his property, the shape slowly disappeared.

The interesting thing about this shape, aside from the fact that it shouldn't have been there, was the color. Being out in the country, it's very dark in his yard. There are no lights in that area of his land. This shape had a definite white color and dense shape to it. It almost seemed to give off its own glow as it made its way to wherever it was going. To this day, Brian has no way to explain what it was he saw that night.

Thankfully for the couple, the miscarriage didn't discourage them about someday having a family. They were eventually able to have two children and because of that, they did some work to their home by adding on an addition. There was one day when Brian was playing with one of their kids in the playroom that was added on to the house. He was lying on the floor and out of the corner of his eye, about two feet away, he saw a pair of black dress shoes and a pair of pants standing completely still. When he followed the legs upward to see who it was, whatever it was disappeared. Unfortunately, he wasn't able to discover who it was because he didn't get past the knees before it withered away.

The spirit here has been known to be helpful as well. Brian used to do some work down in his late father in-laws workshop periodically. The shop was an area where a lot of time was spent mending broken things as well as butchering deer. One hunting season Brian was down in the shop working on setting tables up so they would be ready to go as soon as he got a deer. As he was putting the table together he realized he was going to have to replace a specialized pin that held part of the table together. Unfortunately, he had sheered it off when he was trying to insert it. His father in-law had tons of extra pieces all over in the shop, but no matter how hard

Brian looked, he couldn't locate another one. Frustrated he couldn't finish the task, he went home to see what it would take to order another one.

After having difficulty finding a place where he could order one of these pins, Brian decided to go back down to the workshop the following day to see try and look again. When he entered into the shop, one of the pins he needed to find was laying right in the middle of the table he had been working on. There was no way he could have missed since he had to set up the table to fasten everything into place. The table was empty because of that. He was the only one who knew that the table still needed the pin to stabilize it. He knew immediately that his father in-law placed the missing piece on the table for him to find. Just like most guys, he had an organized mess. He knew exactly where it was even though Brian couldn't locate it.

As I am writing this story, the most recent activity the family has experienced involves their bathroom. The shower curtains have a tendency to open on their own. The first time it happened, they thought that maybe it was caused by one of the kids, but it would also happen when the kids weren't home. My first thought was that perhaps it was a family pet playing with the curtain, but that was quickly denied because they keep the doors shut to the bathroom so the pets couldn't enter.

Sometimes the curtain would open while they were actually in it (cue the Psycho theme) and other times it would open by itself when the family was in the other room. Generally, when it opened, it wouldn't just be opened a couple inches either. It would be opened about 75% of the way thus showing the concerned shower patron in all their glory.

Due to the family having concerns about an investigation doing more harm than good, the family elected to just tell me their story and pass on the thought of us conducting an investigation. I can definitely understand the concerns they have. If you read my book "Lights Out", I have a chapter about how some of the paranormal shows on television are hurting the field. I know this family watches a lot of these shows so they have a misconception of how investigations go down. It is their house though, and as much as I'd love to look into the home more, I do have to respect their decision.

SPIRITS IN THE WINDOW

If you read my last book, *Ghosts Never Say Boo*, you may recall a story I dazzled you with about a young boy being terrorized by what he called a red ghost and a blue ghost. The red ghost was mean and the blue ghost was nice. That was until the spirits found out the big bad ghost investigators were coming. Then the red ghost became nice and told the boy to have the investigators kill the blue ghost. Keeping this story in mind, I became very interested when I received a message about a haunted house dealing with...you guessed it, a red and blue ghost.

By appearance, the home would not have been one that you would think would be haunted. This plays off the title of this book a bit, as you can't always judge a haunted location by appearance alone. There are some houses that look straight out of a horror film, and yet they are lacking the much-expected ghosts. Then there are homes that were built recently, and they are very active. This was one of the homes that would have to be at the low end of the creepy factor. Especially with the big, blowup Minion in the front yard. It was Halloween, and this was part of the display, but it did not cause us to run with our tails between our legs.

I had it set up for us to investigate the home in early October. It took us quite a while to find a date that worked with my schedule since I had just gone through a big career move and had to focus on that before I could work on my hobby. The night that we went to the house, the home owner Jamie was going to be gone getting her kids' haircut. She made me aware of this and said that she would leave the side door unlocked for us and we could just go in and do what we had to do. She was actually only going to be a couple minutes away, so we didn't have very long to go through the couch cushions and look for loose change.

This investigation was conducted by myself, Len and Chasidy. These are characters that I am sure you are aware of if you have followed my career at all. Upon entering the property, we began getting our equipment ready and made ourselves at home. I went into her son's bedroom to set up a video camera and let it start recording while we waited for Jamie to come home. After just a few minutes of being alone in the house, she came walking in with her two boys in tow.

As with any investigation, I like to start the night off by getting some of the ghostly stories. Jamie sat on the floor holding her littlest one while her four-year-old son Brandon played with his toys. I knew from previous conversations that most of the activity occurred around Brandon, so it was good he was around us. Chasidy was in the living room with us taking notes and Len was wondering around. He went into the kitchen area, so hard telling what he ate, or possibly drank. He tends to wonder off a lot, he'll tell us it's to get a feel for the place. I think it's just because he gets confused and doesn't remember where he's at half the time.

One of the earliest memories Jamie had of the events in the home was with her son who was two, going on three at the time. Quite often, at night, he would wake up screaming. This would be followed by him running, crawling or just scrambling to get out of his bedroom. He then would run into his parent's room and jump into bed with them. The first time this happened, Jamie said it was like fireworks with the screams and how fast he came out of the room and how far she jumped out of the bed.

Sometimes Brandon would ask his mom what Zane was doing in his room. Zane is his cousin, and when he would ask this, of course Zane would never have been there. When Jamie would tell him Zane isn't here, he would then ask something to the extent of who's that boy then? He was thinking this boy he was seeing in the house was his cousin because he looked similar.

After seeing this little boy, usually as nothing more than a shadow, Brandon refused to sleep in that room. The family even had concerns that perhaps the local, backwoods, creepy neighbors were maybe looking in their son's window. Most of the times the ghost was seen by the boy, it was in the window, so it was a possibility. Due to this, the family even filed a report with the police in case it was the neighbors.

After countless nights of their son waking up screaming, it really began to take its toll on Jamie. She was pregnant with her second child at this point and sleep was very much needed. Unfortunately, sleep was becoming very difficult to acquire due to these nightly interruptions.

Something was going to have to give, and she was willing to do whatever she needed to do to get some normalcy back into the household. They decided to turn one of their spare rooms into a new bedroom for Brandon. This was probably going to happen eventually anyway, so it was inevitable with their growing family. After completing the new bedroom, the family finally got back to sleeping through the night. Of course, nothing lasts forever.

Months later, Brandon started to have similar experiences in his new room. He became very frightened by something yet again. Much like his old room, he did not want to be in his new room either. When he would have these encounters with whatever was in his room, he would come barreling out of the room trembling all over.

One evening Jamie and Brandon ran some errands and ended up buying some crosses from a local store. When they pulled into their driveway, Brandon began sobbing and crying, saying that he didn't want to go into the house. This affected Jamie because she hated to see her child so scared. It was at this time that he actually told his mom he is seeing ghosts in his room. The idea of ghosts had never been addressed when he was having these encounters. This is something that he came up with on his own. For him only being four years old, that's interesting that he was able to grasp that idea.

When describing the ghosts, Brandon would refer to them by their colors. I am sure you guessed which two colors he used. Red. Blue.

Prior to putting the crosses up in the house, the newborn baby would wake up at 4:30 every morning. The family often wondered if something was waking the baby up or if it was just its natural clock. However, after putting the crosses up in the house, the baby no longer woke up at that time. Jamie did mention that one time when she was showering, a cross fell off the wall in Brandon's room. Perhaps both of these occurrences were nothing more than a coincidence though.

Brandon said the ghost usually likes to hide in the hallway between his bedroom door and the bathroom door. For us investigators, there really wasn't a hiding place there since it was just a flat wall. So, if this was the hiding spot, he would have to be hiding in the walls which definitely wouldn't be unheard of. I think about that all the time when hearing knocking on walls. Is it the sound of spirits communicating with us? Or are they knocking from inside the walls to get our attention so we can let them out.

The ghost would be hiding in between the two doors on the right. Leaning up against the wall is one of my biggest fans. Funny, aren't I?

Brandon also mentioned that the ghost likes to chase the ladies. Well, he didn't really put it that way. I am taking artistic license on this one. He actually said the ghost likes to chase his mom and the family babysitter. The prey never knows they are being chased, but Brandon is able to see it happening.

Most of the experiences seemed to go through Brandon. One time Jamie did hear the sound of toys being played with coming from the bedroom. That wasn't possible though because the kids were all asleep. Jamie's husband hasn't experienced anything, or if he has, he hasn't talked about it to anyone. Other times the sounds

Brandon's Room

of heavy footsteps have been heard coming through the baby monitor

Early one morning Brandon was sitting at the dining room table eating donuts. Jamie was in another room and overheard him offering a donut to someone. Thinking that her husband had walked into the room, Jamie approached Brandon and found him holding a donut up into the air as if offering it to someone who wasn't there.

After finally having enough with all the activity and the lack of sleep everyone was getting, Jamie reached out to her pastor to have the house blessed. Her pastor came out and did her thing. It turns out the pastor actually has some Native American ties, which in my opinion would be perfect for a blessing. I feel this way because I think that what's haunting this home is tied to the land more than the house.

During the blessing, Brandon told the pastor where the spirit was. Brandon went into his old bedroom, which is now the youngest boy's room, and got down on the floor. He then pointed under the chair that stood in the corner and said the ghost was under there. With that, the pastor focused a bit more of her blessing in that area much to the approval of Brandon.

After the blessing, things seemed to calm down quite a bit. The house was calm, Brandon was calm, and everyone was sleeping much better. Brandon didn't mention seeing anything for quite some time afterwards. He was still scared to go into his room or his brother's room by himself though. He said it was still scary in those rooms. I'd take saying a room is scary over saying that he's seeing ghosts any day though. There's a big difference between those two things.

Even if he did eventually go into one of the rooms, he refused to have the blinds closed. This seems really strange though as you would think if he was scared, he would want the blinds closed. That way if something was outside looking into the window, he wouldn't be able to see it. Maybe the ghosts told him to leave it open so they can watch him. That's a thought I don't even like to mention.

One very strange thing happened when Brandon found out we were coming out to the house. Brandon and Jamie were in the family car on the way home from daycare one day. The topic of us coming out to investigate the house came up and Brandon told his mom that the ghosts said they were going to try and kill her. This wasn't a comment that would have ever come out of her son's mouth. It was the Halloween season though, so she felt maybe he overheard something, and used it at home. Maybe some other kids at daycare were talking about their mom. If that's the case, that's a tough little day care.

All of these stories came from Jamie, with a few additions from Brandon periodically thrown in. I did address him directly though on a few occasions. I asked

Brandon's drawing of what the ghost looks like.

him if the ghosts were ever mean to him but he said they were always nice. They usually just talked to him and would ask him if they could play with his toys.

I always like to try and have the kids draw what the ghost looks like too. So, we had him do that at one point during the interview. Very seldom do you see the ink flow from a child's hands as effortlessly as we did that night. Keep in mind this is a four-year old's drawing, so you have to use your imagination a bit. When asked what he wears. Brandon said he wears costumes like Ninja Turtles.

After getting the stories, I decided to poke around a bit in the house. Len had gone outside just to look at the windows to see if something could make the appearance of a person looking in, or if lights could play tricks. There were headlights that could possibly reflect on the windows, so we did have that as a possible explanation. As far as someone peering into the windows, that may have been a little more difficult because the yard was fenced in and the windows weren't easily reachable.

I went down the hall to turn off the hallway light so it wouldn't affect the camera I had running in the bedroom. Just as I was turning it out I noticed that the red light wasn't showing on my camera. Thinking I didn't hit record making the standby power off, I checked the camera out and realized the battery went dead. The battery was a six-hour battery and when I set it up, it had four hours of power. So how did it run out then? Maybe the ghosts needed that energy more than my camera. It turned out upon reviewing the footage; it only recorded for about 30 minutes before the battery went dead.

After dismantling the camera and putting it away, I then went into the first bedroom where most of the experiences occurred. While standing in the room for a few minutes, I did hear a bang coming from the back corner where that chair was. I wondered if I maybe caused it by stepping on a floor board. The room was carpeted, but that doesn't always cover the sound of creaking floor boards. I tried to recreate the sound, but came up empty.

Eventually all three of us ended up in that room to do an EVP session. We had Len on the dowsing rods, Chasidy on the Ghost Radar and me on the K2. Sounds like a paranormal rock band, doesn't it? I was asking a ton of questions. We didn't get anything on audio, but we did get some possible interaction visibly.

For the dowsing, we were getting some answers, but they didn't seem consistent enough to really consider them as positive evidence. As far as the K2 meter, the interaction was quite a bit better. When we would ask the spirits to make the lights go to red, it generally would.

Of all the tools, we used during the investigation, I think the Ghost Radar may have been our best tool for the night. At one point during our EVP session, we asked if there was anyone with us right now and the word "evidence" came up. We repeated the question again, and the word "uncle" came up. Of course, we asked Jamie if an uncle could be haunting the house, but she said no.

All three of us had the app running at some point during the night. When we compared all the words between us, there was a common theme that we found.   A lot of words were tied to the ground. We received words like land, acres, lake, garden and farm. So, that makes me kind of wonder if it's the ground and not the house that's haunted as stated before.

All and all, it was a very quiet night for us with the investigation.   I am hopeful for the family that the blessing that was done a month before we came out, did its job and the spirits have moved on. I did reach out to Jamie again before writing this article to see if there's been any more activity since we left and there has been. Her son hasn't been experiencing anything though, it's actually all been experienced by Jamie now.   Almost nightly she is hearing footsteps coming into her bedroom. She wakes up thinking it's Brandon, and of course, there's nobody there.

Seems like one of those stains you just can't rid of. This one may take a few cleansings.

HAUNTING OF A RIVER TOWN

I always try to keep my locations secret for various reasons. It has nothing to do with me not wanting to share a ghostly honey hole or anything like that. It's mainly just to keep some of the crazy paranormal people from bothering those who were kind enough to let me investigate their home or business. However, this story will be a bit different as they were completely open to me disclosing the location we were investigating. This location is the Nicholas Sauer Memorial Building in Evansville, IL. The beauty of being able to give out the site also allows me to give the reader more accurate history of the location. Plus, I don't have to get creative with making up names for those involved so I have that going for me as well. Of course, before I get into the town's history, I have to do my usual storytelling. I feel it's the stories like these that set my books apart from other ghost books. It's more personable and you get to know me a bit more and hopefully have a chuckle along the way.

When I was a kid I spent a lot of time down near Evansville. My grandpa owned a fishing clubhouse that was within walking distance of the Kaskaskia River. I loved going on these fishing trips with him. My grandpa was crazy and if my mom knew some of the stuff he did with us, she would have freaked out. My mom can't swim and I really think that she thinks not being able to swim is hereditary. So, if she can't swim, then that lack of skill was passed down to her kids through her genes. I can tell her I was wading in a knee-high creek exploring and she'll ask if I was wearing a lifejacket.

For some reason, my grandpa thought the fishing on the other side of the Kaskaskia River would be far better than the side we were on. So, he would throw my two brothers and I into his little row boat and then he'd start rowing like a mad man to get across the river. If we only had a drum to beat on to help him keep his rowing rhythm. You had to row quickly because of all the barges that traveled that stretch. You did not want to be caught in the middle of a huge river in a little boat when one of those barges went by.

We would then tie off to a tree on the other side of the river and tight line for catfish. That was my grandpa's main method of fishing. I remember gripping the boat very tightly when the barges would come because we would be bouncing up and down from the waves caused by the massive coal and grain toting barges. We caught tons of fish, some quite large, before we'd start the gauntlet of getting back across the river again.

Here's one other fond story that will hopefully make you laugh a bit. One early morning we headed out to the clubhouse and just as we were approaching the turnoff between Ruma and Evansville, it began to pour down rain. When we arrived to the clubhouse we actually stayed in the car to wait out the storm. Finally, it stopped and we grabbed our gear and headed down to one of the lakes that were also on location. I was probably around six years old at the time. I need to make that clear so you can better understand my thought process with what I was about to do.

Due to all the rain, the trek to the lake was very muddy and treacherous. When I got down to the spot where we were going to throw our lines in, I figured I should probably clean the mud off my shoes. Now, the logical thing to have done would be to grab one of the abundant sticks that lay at my feet and use that to scrape off the mud. Not me though, I wanted to be creative and have fun while doing it. So, I instead decided to start kicking my foot out into the air. Scientifically this worked great. The force that I was using along with the abrupt stop that my foot would make when it reached its limit of flexibility would thereby cause the mud and dirt to continue in the direction of my movement which meant the debris would be deposited into the lake. Not only that, but it would also make things splash in the water, which is music to the ears of a six-year-old.

All of this worked great until the basis of my theory proved true on more than just the dirt that riddled my sneakers. Mixed in with the melody of the small chunks of dirt splashes came a crescendo of a much larger splash. Then came the sad reality of me looking down and realizing I only had one shoe on as the other was now resting in Davy Jones Locker. Not only was I shoeless, I also had to tell my grandpa what happened which was even scarier to me. So, what was a six-year-old to do? Easy, lie! Or rather, stretch the truth a bit. Maybe a rabid beaver tore it off my foot. Perhaps I was standing too close to a crawfish hole and one came out grabbing my shoe with his pinchers as he backed down his hole. I needed to stick with the truth and stretch some other aspect to save my hide.

I did tell him exactly how it happened; there was no denying the truth there. He was my grandpa; I at least owed him that. But to lessen the blow, I told him the shoe only landed a few feet out into the lake when in all actuality; it flew a good 15 to 20 feet into the lake. The stretching of the truth backfired though because he made me shimmy out on a log into the lake to try and retrieve the shoe. So here I am, on a log, in a shark infested lake (when I fished there, I was convinced I was going to catch a shark), knowing all too well that my shoe was nowhere near the search perimeter I was assigned.

Walking around in one shoe, one muddy sock, soaked pants and having my grandpa upset with me was only the beginning. We didn't have much money in my family in those days, and now I was going to need a new pair of shoes. To teach me a lesson, my mom had me pay for my own shoes with my birthday money which is the last thing I wanted to spend that money on. That money would have been better used for Star Wars toys. What lesson did I learn from this event? Be honest with my grandpa? Don't always look for the easiest and quickest way to solve a problem? To appreciate and take care of what I have? Nope, the lesson I learned was to make sure to double knot my shoes so the next time I karate kick dirt off my shoes, they would not fly off again.

Let's get back on task now with the ghostly story. Years ago, I spoke at a library in Evansville, IL. The building labeled my little segment as "A Haunting of a River Town" which was a pretty cool title. I unfortunately felt bad about this because none of the stories I was presenting on were about that area. The building was cool and the employees there were wonderful. The event had me doing two separate presentations in the actual library, and ended with a hay ride out to a local cemetery at night. All of this was also accompanied by a cookout which consisted of some incredibly tasty chili! I figured with all the chili people ate, we would probably see some gaseous forms at some point during the evening. Although it may be followed by a smell resembling death, it would be easily debunked and deemed not paranormal due to the intake of said chili.

One interesting thing happened at the cemetery that evening. This also shows how one cannot say that all orbs are spirit energy. It also shows how the camera can mislead us. During the cemetery walkthrough, a patron came up to me excitedly with their camera in hand. With their hands shaking, they showed me their photo. In the image, you can see a tombstone about 6 feet away and floating above the marker was a perfectly round ball of light. Of course, the photographer knew immediately that it had to of been a ghost, and to be honest, I was on the "ghost" side of the fence myself. I gave them my email and had them email it to me for further inspection.

Upon returning home and looking at the image a bit more closely, I discovered that the orb was not an orb at all. In fact, when zooming in on the shape, it wasn't even close to being a ball shape. It actually turned out to be a bug. You could see the wings and its little feet hanging down at the bottom. It was strange how when looking at it from the original distance it had one shape, and then took on a whole different shape the closer you get to it. After discovering what it was, I then had the difficult task of letting the person know that it was not a ghost. This is always tough because people want to think their evidence is always something paranormal. Now, I am also creative enough to give them something else to chew on as well so they wouldn't be completely let down, and I was going to exercise that ability with this case. I contacted the person and told them that it definitely was not a ghost. What they captured was actually some kind of flying insect. I also offered the suggestion that it could quite possibly be a "fairy" due to the wings and the little legs and feet. For all I know, it could have been showering us with pixie dust as well. So now we may have fairies inhabiting Evansville, IL. Who would have thought?

I guess the first visit I made as a speaker went over well because they did have me back a second time. Although thoughts of them not doing a cookout were tossed around, I insisted that there be chili. And well....

The Nicholas Sauer Memorial Building
(Photo by Bethany Wunderlich)

there was chili! That was my form of payment for speaking back then. Let me sell my books and feed me chili.

During my speaking engagements at the building I was given some history of the location and was also told of some of the ghostly encounters they have had at the building. I never did an investigation there, but the stories were still in the back of my mind for years after the events I had there. Then, as I began work on this book, I started to think about some possible locations I could write about that haven't been done before. Since I still kept in touch with Bethany, the one who brought me out there to speak, I thought I would ask her if I could come out and investigate. She reached out to the mayor and very quickly returned to me with a yes! A date was set for the investigation and all was right in the world. I was returning to the building that helped me very early on as I began to get more and more comfortable speaking in front of people. I could not wait to go back!

Time for some history! Evansville officially became a village in 1885, but the area was most likely inhabited much earlier than that. There is evidence of Native American's in the area, which will of course pre-date any white men from settling in the area, but we'll focus on some of the people who were more involved in what the city is today. Some of the earliest known settlers go back to the early 1800's when a gentleman by the name of Alexander Clark started a farm in the area. He was followed by another settler named John Campbell a couple years later. Who in turn was followed by a couple more settlers until eventually Cadwell Evans began to set the groundwork for the village of Evansville when he sectioned off the area into streets and home sites.

Although the Kaskaskia River had already been widely used for transportation, in 1866, Philip Sauer purchased a milling company along the river with his son Nicholas which helped usher in the commercial use of the river. Upon new ownership, the mill became known as the N & P Milling Company. I assume that stands for Nicholas & Philip Milling Company. It helped move the area into an important age with the transportation of grain via barges that the river still sees to this day. The mill also brought the technology of a roller system to Southern IL. A roller mill generally uses 2-6 rollers that are cylindrical in shape and move back and forth to grind or crush materials. One can also adjust the distance between the rollers in order to crush materials into smaller pieces. These are used for grains, rocks, etc. Output at the mill doubled and tripled through the years and provided some of the finest flour in the area. Eventually the Mill became the N & W Sauer Mill when Nicholas' brother William took over for his father. In

Nicholas Sauer

1899, the mill was incorporated as the Sauer Milling Company.

Through the years, the Sauer family became a very prominent part of the development of Evansville and the surrounding area. The patriarch Philip originally came to the United States from Germany. He found his way to the Midwest via New Orleans and he made his way up the Mississippi to St. Louis. He later settled near Red Bud where he was a Justice of the Peace and the Treasurer. He passed away in 1892 at the age of eighty-three.

Nicholas, born in 1831, was a wonderful person who did everything he could for the betterment of the village of Evansville. He was an honest man who earned everything through hard work and dedication. He married Virginian Elizabeth Gerlache in 1866. They had five children together named John, Magdalena, Philip, William and George. Nicholas played a vital role in bringing the railroad to Evansville, starting the Evansville Bank and building a bridge across the Kaskaskia. With his business sense and financial prowess, there was a promising political career in his future if he so desired. Although he was nominated to run as a Republican for the Illinois Senator Ticket, Nicholas passed on this opportunity.

Nicholas died on October 21st, 1908 brought on by an accident at his home. Unfortunately, three days earlier, Nicholas was on the front porch of his home during the evening. Someone had mistakenly left open a trap door that leads down to the cellar of the home. Nicholas, not noticing this void, fell through the opening and sustained internal injuries

Photo of Magdalena that hangs in the foyer of the building.

from the fall. These injuries brought on his untimely death a few days later.

Forty years later in 1949, his daughter Magdalena erected the Nicholas Sauer Memorial Building in honor of her late father. The building is located at 403 Spring Street and is currently the home of the town library, city hall and police & fire station. There's also a small park in the back of the building where children can come and play.

When we received the green light to do the investigation at the building, the only stipulation was that the mayor Craig and his wife Monica, and Bethany and her husband Rob, were allowed to be present during the investigation. I was more than happy to allow that. They were all interested in ghost stories and had their share of experiences inside the building. Sometimes having familiar faces at an investigation can help trigger activity for us. If the spirits are comfortable around certain individuals, maybe they will be less shy about making an appearance. We just have to be careful that the investigation doesn't turn into a party where we end up being followed around everywhere we go by an entourage.

Making the trek to Evansville for the investigation was myself, Len and Chasidy. Originally, we were going to have Julie come with us, but she had to back out due to illness. We met at my house at 7pm and were on our way with the hopes of arriving by 8pm. Sometimes my wife rubs off on me though and I somehow become late, as was the case with this investigation. We ended up arriving about ten minutes late which I despise. It's my fault as I forgot how far of a drive that actually was for me. Having a long drive like that though gave me an opportunity to give Chas and Len some info about the location. When we finally arrived, Bethany met us outside and in we went.

After some brief introductions, we began getting bombarded with stories. I came in after everyone else since I was pulling the cart of equipment, and when I got situated, the stories were already flying so I had to quickly get out my digital recorder so I could capture them. As I collected the stories, we were also getting a tour. These are some of the shared experiences they are having in the building.

The first area we went to was the basement. The basement had changed a lot since the last time I was there. The way I remembered it was coming down some stairs, seeing the two jail cells and then seeing a huge pile of boxes that impeded any further advancement. This time, I could have done somersaults, if they didn't make me dizzy due to my old age, in the wide-open space beyond the cells. The whole area had been organized and which definitely opened the space up.

Bethany didn't like coming down to the basement because of an encounter she had a while back. It wasn't because of some deranged, formerly incarcerated specter; it was something even more sinister. Bethany came in contact with a brown recluse spider in one of the cells. By contact, I mean the spider's ferocious fangs met Bethany's skin. As Bethany stated, she won't go in there because it hurts when you get bit.

There weren't very many stories from the basement I think mainly because there is no need for people to spend much time down there. Law of averages, the less you frequent a location, the fewer chances of having an experience. There was one good story that was shared with us though from this area. Years ago, one of the new police officers had an experience in lower level. He came into the building one day and heard someone rooting around in the basement. On edge, he drew his gun and began creeping down the steps so he could get the drop on the perp. As he made his way into the basement, he found himself completely alone. There was no sign of anyone, nor did he hear the noise that brought him down there in the first place. Scared, he then ran back up the stairs and out of the building frightened by what he didn't see. After wrapping up the stories in the basement, we eventually made our way back up to the main level.

On the first floor, when Bethany would be working at her desk, she would hear the sound of someone walking back and forth in the library on the second floor. Although usually it just sounded like someone casually moving about, other times it would sound like children were playing. Sounds of the kids running from one end of the library to the other were definitely out of place. Sometimes she would even hear the sound of muffled voices. The library is only open two days a week on Tuesdays and Thursdays, and these sounds would occur all days of the week. It seems as though the spirits felt the hours of the library operation didn't apply to them.

I inquired about any kind of water pipes that could be in the floor, but that was quickly knocked out of the equation, because there weren't any water pipes. I then thought maybe it was the ductwork for the heating and cooling, but up until last year, they didn't even have central air up there. So, there is really no explanation to what's making the sounds. Generally, when investigating a place where there are stories of footsteps on a second floor, it can usually be debunked by locating pipes and ducts. This was not the case here.

Other times when Bethany would be hard at work, she would be interrupted by the door to her office being opened by some unseen force. Bethany would then call out to Magdalena and inform her that they need to keep the door closed, and like clockwork, the door would slowly begin to close.

Craig came in to work early one morning before everyone else as usual and was surprised to hear several people had beat him there that morning. As he came through the main door, he heard a conversation coming from the conference room. The conversation had at least three different people taking part. He made his way across the reception area and opened the door to the conference room and found himself completely alone. He knew he heard people in there, but they simply vanished. When I asked him if he could tell what they were saying, he said he unfortunately wasn't able to decipher it. He could tell there were three different voices for sure though.

The closet in the near the reception tends to get a bit active as well. The door that leads to the closet is a very tough door to open and shut. It sticks and often takes some elbow grease to get it to work properly. One day the door opened up on its own and then quickly slammed shut. The speed at which it closed was so quick that tons of papers were blown off the bulletin board that hangs near the closet door.

We then headed up to the 2nd floor where the library is located. I was hoping when we walked up the stairs we would see a ghostly librarian telling us to shhh, but we came up empty on that one. Even though I was let down with the ghostly image, the stories the building staff experienced up there were just as exciting.

Bethany's husband Rob went to the library one day to check out a book about the history of Evansville. This book is guarded by the library as it's a great, rare book all about the beginnings of the village. Rob carried it to the librarian's desk and set it down on the table. They began to find themselves engaged in a conversation of some sort for about fifteen minutes. When the conversation ended, Rob reached for the book so he could check it out and found his hand grabbing at an empty desk. The book was gone. They looked all over the desk and after several minutes found the book returned to its original resting spot on the shelf. There was no way someone could have returned the book because something like that would have been noticed. The book was returned by something far greater than what our minds could comprehend.

After we got this story, I felt like it was time to do an experiment. I wanted to get the book and put it on the librarian's desk to see if it would return itself to the shelf again. Unfortunately, we were unable to even locate the book. In fact, there was a sign at the desk stating that this book was not allowed to leave the building. While we were trying to find the book, the Ghost Radar decided to talk to us. It said the word "case". We found

Library aisles look a lot creepier with a full spectrum camera.

out later that the library keeps the book locked up until someone wants to view it.   Later that night my radar said "secret" and "key" within a couple minutes of each other in the library area.   Whether or not these three words pertained to the book is really up in the air.   The words do relate to how protected the book is.

One day the fire chief had to pick up some papers up in the library.   When he got up there, he grabbed the papers off the desk and as he began to read them, he started hearing someone breathing right behind him.   It was very loud and heavy breaths that seemed to be coming down on him.   It was almost as if someone was looking over his shoulder reading the papers along with him.   Frightened, he turned around very quickly and found that there was nobody behind him.   Not able to bear it any longer, he stormed back down the stairs and refused to go back up there again.

One time when Bethany was up in the library dropping off some paperwork during off hours, she saw a swish of a skirt near the stage at the far end of the library. There's a bannister that runs along one side of the stage and this skirt seemed to flutter near that. She made her way to a location where she could get a better view of the bannister, but didn't see anyone over there. She said "Hi Magdalena" and then made her way back downstairs in a quick, swift manner.

When Craig's wife Monica was in high school, she helped fill in at the library every once in a while. Her mother convinced her that all she had to do was sit there and do nothing since nobody ever came in to the library in those days. With that in mind, it was definitely easy money for a broke high school student. Knowing now that all the sounds she heard while she was sitting there alone doing nothing, were probably caused by the building's ghostly inhabitants, she has a big "hell no" for her ever doing that again. She feels the $10 for cigarette money would definitely not have been worth it if she knew what was really causing the sounds.

I asked Bethany how she would rank the three floors from most active to least active and it goes like this. The library seems to be the most active. Whether it is the sounds that occur very frequently, books moving about and even glimpses of apparitions, they all make it an easy choice for the top spot. Following in second place is the first floor. Here's where conversations could be heard, doors opening and closing and of course hearing the noises coming from the library. Winning the Bronze Medal, would be the basement with its noises and terrifying arachnids.

After the story telling segment was over, we began to set up our equipment. I really wanted to set up my video camera in the basement aiming at the two cells. The doors were open to them, so I was hoping to have some kind of movement occur with them. I also set up a laser grid on the floor aiming past the cell doors, with the hopes of capturing shadows or other types of movement. Unfortunately, with my infrared extender active, the lights from the grid were all but drowned out. I could really only make out a handful of them, but I still left it on just in case the spirits would become interested in the pretty lights.

Once the camera was set up, I walked by the cell doors just to look at them, and then turned out the lights. I then walked back to the camera so I could check the quality of the image with the infrared. Just as I looked through the viewfinder, I did spot a bright white light coming towards me. I quickly hit record, but it was gone at that point. Frustrated because I didn't know if I was able to capture it, I ended up convincing myself that it was probably just dust anyway. I then made my way back upstairs to the main lobby to meet up with everyone.

I had my ghost radar sitting on the front desk in the reception area while I was in the basement. I looked at it just to see if any words came through and very interestingly I got the word "hold" at 8:47:44 pm. At 8:48:11 I got the word "cell"! What are the odds of that? Here I am setting up video camera in the room that still houses the original jail cells, and I get "hold" and "cell". What really makes this a coincidence is these cells were not your long-term cells. These cells were mainly used when park visitors were getting a bit unruly. They would "hold" them in these "cells" until their tempers cooled down a bit or until the alcohol began to wear off. Although not the same in appearance, they reminded me of the Andy Griffith Show and having them be used by the town drunk. Already some potential evidence and we were just moments into the investigation.

Len was sitting in the conference room getting his new camera system up and running. This was going to be the first time he used it on an investigation and I was quite impressed how easily he was able to operate it. I had some concern when he told me he was going to use it on this investigation because he typically uses what I would deem "old school" investigative equipment. Things like flatbed tape recorders, older video cameras, dowsing rods, etc. are usually his weapons of choice. When he told me he was bringing this higher tech set up, I mentioned that he may want to try and familiarize himself with it before we get to the investigation as to avoid not looking professional in front of the building staff. Aside from one of the camera's infrared being faulty, it went without a hitch.

I was in charge of setting the cameras up while he monitored my proposed angles from the monitor screen. At first, we were using our cell phones to talk back and forth, but we soon realized we could do the same thing by yelling. So, we began yelling back and forth until the cameras were in the perfect positions. We placed one of the three cameras in the basement, and the other two were aiming towards opposite ends of the library. Len also set up a digital camera in the conference room where the monitor viewing station was located.

While I was setting up the cameras in the library, Chasidy had an encounter with a bit of a frisky ghost. She was taking notes throughout the evening on her trusty notepad. At one point, she set the notepad down on a table and leaned over to write on it. All of a sudden, she felt something bump into her from behind, she stood up and turned around only to find nobody was there. Thinking she just imagined it, she leaned over again to finish her thought and yet again, she was bumped in to. At this point she was pretty freaked out and ran over to Craig and me, telling us what she had just experienced.

Moments after that, Craig and I were talking and we heard a loud bang come from the northeast corner of the library. Craig and I both looked in the direction of the sound and then at each other. After confirming we both heard the noise, I asked him if that was a normal sound. He said it wasn't so we began to inspect where the sound came from. We didn't hear it again, and furthermore, found no source for what may have caused it. Another interesting thing happened with the ghost radar at this point. After the sound, I made reference to finding out if Craig heard the sound? Immediately after I asked the question, the word "listen" popped up. Then the word "bigger" immediately followed. When we turned around from investigating the source of the sound to start to head back to the first floor, the word "caught" came up. Perhaps the spirit was telling us to listen for a bigger sound and then realized we caught it. Maybe I am pulling at straws, but it makes sense.

Chasidy had an interesting encounter during this short amount of time up in the library. Chasidy was within days of needing to turn in all her final work to graduate from college. She was responsible for making a portfolio and then adding to it as she finished her assignments. Chasidy and the members of her group should have been working on it for two years, but they were still scrambling as the end drew near. Including Chasidy, there were a total of eight students in the group. They utilize a group text so they can ask each other questions on assignments which worked quite well and was pretty efficient. As Chasidy was sitting at a table in the library monitoring the Ghost Radar, her phone vibrated to let her know she had a text. One of her fellow classmates was asking about a part of the portfolio that she was having issues with. Chasidy answered her text and went back to ghost radar. When she turned it back on, the first word that appeared was "pupil".

With all the cameras rolling we decided to congregate up in the library and do an EVP session. It was Me, Chasidy, Len, Bethany and Craig. Monica and Rob decided to stay on the first floor in the reception area. We all sat around a table with the digital recorders, ghost radar and K2's running. Len was using his dowsing rods as a means of communicating as well.

At one point, I went down to the basement to retrieve my Laser Grid so we could use it during the EVP session. Upon returning to the library, as I got back to the table, I noticed this black shape out of the corner of my eye. It wasn't a full-figured kind of apparition, but more of a sliver for lack of a better word. When it happened, I mentioned to everyone that I had just seen a black shape and Len said that he also saw something in the same spot and at the same moment that I did. It was almost like a rope that was hanging right next to me. It was not very thick at all and it was also kind of wavy as it stretched vertically. I am not sure how long it was, as I only saw it out of the corner of my eye.

I like to use a tripod to stabilize my laser grid. Not only does it hold it steady, but it also holds the button mechanism in place on the piece so that the grid will stay on. Len, not knowing about this device asked how I keep it on. I began to explain how the tripod has a hole in it and when you stick the laser grid into the hole it turns it on. Now, to better illustrate how it works, I was also using my right hand and making an opening with my thumb and index finger. This was to help represent what the tripod opening looked like. Then, I used my left-hand index finger and made it stick out straight to represent the laser grid. Then, I slowly moved the left-hand finger into the opening, back and forth to show how to insert it. Of course, with this visual display, and the explanation of sticking it in to turn it on, and with it being very late, we all of a sudden burst out into a ton of laughter. If you aren't laughing already, please re-read the paragraph and use your imagination.

Since some of the employees of the building feel the spirit of Magdalena may be the prominent ghost they have experienced, a lot of our questions were directed towards her. We did get a little feedback from the dowsing rods. Sometimes the rods would move with vigor and other times, they seemed to be quite lazy.

As we started this session, Len began to explain to the spirits the many ways that they can communicate with us. Whether it was by using the K2 meter, affecting his dowsing rods, communicating through the digital recorder, or any other devices, we were there for them with the hopes of being able to converse. Just as he finished saying this, the Ghost Radar popped up the word "agree".

When we asked if the spirit lived here their whole life, the dowsing rods moved into the "yes" position. At this point the word "wolf" popped up on the radar. Thinking that maybe the person's last name could be Wolf, we did ask that. According to Bethany, Wolfe is a name from the Evansville area. On this, the dowsing rods went to yes as well, but it was a very slow kind of yes.

I tried to do my knocking pattern trick to see if I could get some kind of reaction from the spirits, but I came up empty. When I did the pattern, the dowsing rods crossed, and just then Len started getting cold. He mentions to us that he is getting cold and asks the spirits if they are by him right now. A few seconds after he asks the question, you can hear a male whisper say "I can see it…. see it". Len then mentions that he felt a big shiver go down his back. We took a break shortly after this to adjust some equipment to better pick up any kind of energy.

Listening to the audio now and hearing this whisper, I am almost wondering if it was one of us saying it. I know it wasn't Len or Craig, so the only other male there was me. However, I don't recall saying anything like that during the investigation. Since we had a K2 meter going, it may have been lighting up at the time, and maybe I was saying "I can see it" in confirmation of the K2 lighting up. My only defense for that is if I would have said something like that, I wouldn't have whispered the comment. I would have just come out and said it. There would have been no use whispering a comment like that. So, I cannot say definitively that it was a ghost communicating, but I also can't say that it wasn't.

I was debating about omitting this from the book, but I want to use it as a teaching tool. You could have the greatest evidence in the world, but if you aren't careful, the evidence could be "possibly" explained naturally. Any skeptic will come up with tons of explanations for why something isn't paranormal. As investigators, we need to make sure that none of our evidence is contaminated. If you are about to say something on camera, make sure you make a note on paper or to the equipment that you are the one talking. If you make a bang, mention that. That way later when you are reviewing the evidence, you won't second guess anything that you may have captured. Since there were three guys in this EVP session, that's an easy one to debunk and say it was one of us.

When we reconvened the session, we had Bethany do most of the questioning. Hoping that maybe the familiarity of her voice would possible lure the spirits out was the basis of this decision. When she asked if the spirits were shy, the dowsing rods went to yes again. While she was asking questions, I kept hearing a strange noise outside the second story window. To me it sounded like a wagon going down the street, which would have been awesome! If you've ever seen the movie "*Scrooge*", the musical version of "*A Christmas Carol*" with Albert Finney, there's a scene in the beginning where a ghostly horse drawn carriage roars through Scrooge's home.

That's the vision I had as I ran to the window to check on the ruckus. Of course, there was no wagon, but I did notice how violently the American flag was beating around the flagpole. The flag was right outside our window and it was causing the noises I heard. So, that was obviously debunked. What's funny though is when I came back to the table; the word "horse" came up on the radar.

We asked some other questions such as whether the spirits could move around the building and if the equipment we had was maybe a little too confusing for them to manipulate. Bethany mentioned to the spirits that it may be easier to use the dowsing rods to communicate with us. Len then asked if it was easier to cross the rods to answer as a yes. Just then the rods crossed very quickly and you could actually hear it happen. We all got a kick out of how quickly they moved and had quite the chuckle because of it.

One other thing that happened during this session was very entertaining. At one point a question was asked as to whether or not there were other spirits in the room with us. It was made clear that this wasn't asked because we didn't want to talk to Magdalena any longer; we just wanted to know if there were others. After not getting any kind of response, Len asked if Magdalena was still with us, and within about ten seconds, the word "maybe" popped up on the radar. We all got a kick out of that. It was almost like she was jealous, so she said maybe instead of a yes or no answer.

We decided at this point to take another break and get everyone into the library for one last EVP session. This one was to be conducted at a large table next to the stage. The humor continued because at one point Bethany tried to squeeze by the table and ended up bumping into the table with a pretty solid hip check. As she did this the word "space" and then "fat" came up on the radar. What a strange coincidence that was.

We were getting pretty slap happy at this point in the evening. As we were getting ready to go into serious investigation mode, Bethany told a story about a Dora the Explorer toy they had at their house. It was a kitchen set, and sometimes at night it would turn on and start saying lines from the show. Not only did the voice terrify them, but it got quite annoying too, so they removed the batteries from the item. Oddly enough, the toy would continue to talk even without batteries. Now hearing this story got my creative juices flowing and I started to have my vision of a haunted Dora toy of which I expressed to the others at the table. I was seeing a deranged Dora, with the Chucky sinister look on her face as she raised a huge carving knife into the air and plunged it into an already field dressed Boots (her monkey friend for those that have never seen the show) who lay in front of her. Most likely, she would then say something like "Hola, soy Dora, ¿Quieres jugar?" Translated to English for the non Spanish speaking folks, "Hi, I'm Dora, ¿Wanna play?"

During this session, I broke out the Ghost Radio, but didn't have any success with it. We did use the K2 which was getting some love. At this point the laser grid batteries were dead, so we didn't have access to that any longer. That's been my experience with laser grids though; they seem to blow through batteries. This grid was Len's, although he was using my tripod. The grid that I use has a special attachment that allows it to be plugged into a wall. I highly recommend one of these if you use a laser grid.

All efforts to try and get the spirits to communicate in some shape or form were not successful. We did get a little dowsing communication as well as getting some K2 hits to light up on demand, but that was it. Nothing was real concrete evidence. Bethany did get a major shiver which I noticed as it was happening, but nothing seemed to be going on around her that we could measure. I checked the EMF readings and temperature around her, but it just didn't manipulate the readers. Since it was already getting pretty late, and we felt that the spirits had grown tired of us, we decided to start to wrap up the investigation.

As we were breaking down all of the equipment and trying to put everything back where it belonged, I got attacked by a six-foot-long bench. As I showed it what for and knocked it over using my shin, Monica let out this amazing, Hollywood caliber scream, embedded with some very colorful obscenities. What she thought was something paranormal was actually just my lack of night vision and clumsiness. Her reaction was priceless though.

To close out the investigation, I did want to go into the basement and do a small EVP session when I retrieved mine and Len's cameras. So, Len, Craig and I all went down there for a few minutes. We set up a K2 meter on one of the cell doors and then began asking questions. Although the K2 was lighting up frantically, the audio was lacking any evidence. I kind of wondered if maybe the K2 was getting low on battery power and maybe that was why it was lighting up erratically.

Within the next few weeks I began the tedious task of sifting through all the evidence. Upon reviewing the footage on the video, unfortunately, I wasn't fast enough to capture the orb that was coming toward the camera when I first hit the record button. Although bummed out, I relished in the fact that most likely it was indeed dust that I must have stirred up, so maybe I didn't really miss anything important.

All throughout the video I kept getting these really odd noises. They occurred every ten to fifteen minutes. To me, the noises sounded like a bucket being dropped upside down. It had a hollow kind of ring to it and that was the only thing I could associate it with. I contacted Bethany and told her I had some homework for her. I needed her to go down in the creepy basement when she was alone in the building, to see if she could hear this noise. Luckily, she was game because she was able to not only witness the sound, but also pin down the source. She was able to debunk the noise as being caused by the water heater.

About twelve minutes into the video I did capture what sounds like a person yelling. One has to take this with a grain of salt though unfortunately. There were several people in the building and I do not have voice signatures for each person. So, it may have just been one of us making a noise.

For the next hour or so the video was very dull. I am sure I dozed off a couple times while reviewing it. Sure, it had its usual bucket sounds which I did write down until I could further investigate it, but other than that, it was very quiet. After an hour and fifteen minutes, I did capture another possible voice. This one had a mechanical sound to it. I've captured audio like this before where the voice has a weird sound to it. There were people talking at the same time, but this is at a lower level than the other voices. I haven't been able to decipher what is being said, so maybe you can take a listen to it and figure it out.

A few minutes later there was a sound similar to that of a ball bouncing. This may have been caused by the water heater or one of the other devices in the basement. Ten minutes after that, a strange looking creature made its way down the stairs and into the basement. Naturally, this was only me as I needed to retrieve my laser grid tripod (as mentioned earlier) to use it upstairs during our EVP session.

A minute or so after I left from the basement, another orb made an appearance in the shot. Here's my take on these orb appearances. During the two hours of video I reviewed, the two times I saw an orb on camera was shortly after I walked through the area. So, were these orbs real paranormal phenomenon or just merely dust set in motion by the breeze I caused when walking by? Being a skeptic of orbs, I'd have to think it was dust. But, for two hours, there were only two of them. Usually when I see dust orbs, they are moving around a lot more frequently. Another issue to think about with this one I caught on video, is I am walking away from the camera, and it is moving towards the camera. I would think if it was my motion, then the orb would move in the same direction as I. Lastly, there was a bit of time lapse from when I walked by to when the orb appeared. So, is this orb dust or spirit energy? I wish I had the answer.

Aside from these events, there were quite a few different sounds from creaks to bangs, but I think those were all just natural noises from the old building. With the furnace running, water heater banging, floor boards creaking, traffic driving by and seven people moving about, any sound like that would have to be considered normal.

Along with the video data I had to go through, I also took about eighty to one hundred photographs with my full spectrum digital camera.   Of all those photos, I may have got one photo worth mentioning. I was up in the library by myself. I was snapping photographs all over the area sometimes with an infrared extender and sometimes without. In one particular image, where I did use the extender, you can see a bright white orb in front of one of the chairs. I zoomed in on it and can tell that you are not able to see through this anomaly. It's dense and bright. It could be an orb, it may be dust. As mentioned earlier though, if it were dust, I feel that I

The orb is in front of the four chairs by the far table.

would have seen more of it. It's another one of those pieces of evidence that I have to leave to you to decide.

Although in good company for the evening, the hopes of paranormal activity were a bit more limited than I had envisioned. I do feel the building is haunted; it was just a little quiet for us that night. With the age and history of the town, as well as the river located just blocks from the building, the haunted framework that we would look for is present. Perhaps the spirits were just quiet because they weren't familiar with us. Maybe our gadgets intimidated them and presented an obstacle they weren't willing to overcome to communicate with us. The building definitely wasn't scary. It was very warm and inviting. It's probably one of those haunted buildings where things happen when you aren't actively looking for them.

The scariest part of this whole trip occurred on the way home. We were very hungry and decided to stop at a McDonalds to get something to eat. When we pulled into the parking lot, you could tell the lobby was closed but we were hopeful that the drive thru would still be open. When we pulled up to the menu, we were met with silence. We sat there for a few minutes without a single word coming from the speaker. With no response, I decided to pull up to the first window. Although we could see two employees with their backs to us, they never once turned around. I just kept sitting there staring at the backs of their heads. All they had to do was turn around and say we are closed, and we would have left, but they didn't. I even honked a couple times but it fell on deaf ears.

I desperately needed two all-beef patties on a bun or maybe a quarter-pounder with cheese, so I wasn't going to give up that easy. I pulled up to the second window to see if I could get some much-needed attention there. Although I didn't see any employees, I did see a mouse come out from underneath the sales counter. He then ran back underneath it after I yelled and pointed at it. Len even shrieked and pulled his legs up onto the seat as he danced about with his pantlegs pulled up revealing his shins.

Unlike the actual employees though, the mouse did come back out from under the counter and looked me right in the eye, acknowledging that I was there. I had to pull up a bit so Chasidy, who was sitting in the back seat, was able to see the mouse as well. He then headed over towards the food, I can only assume to get himself a fry or some other late-night morsel. Well, the mouse didn't even have to tell us they were closed for us to make the decision to not eat there that night or probably any other night in the near future. So off we went to try and find another establishment to get a bite to eat. With the late hour though, it ended up with us just having to go home to scavenge.

I am sure patrons of the Nicholas Sauer Memorial Building will eventually come in contact with the spirits that reside in the building. Who it is, we weren't able to find out. But I have no doubts that Magdalena is probably one of the spirits. It was her doing that got the building there in the first place as a way of honoring her late father. Why wouldn't she still be there to make sure that the building is taken care of and treated with the respect she envisioned? After all, it's her family name on the plaque and she has her heritage to protect.

References:

www.mygenealogyhound.com
http://fcihg.genealogyvillage.com/SauerNicholas.html
www.evansville.org

HERE COMES THE JUDGE

       After years of having the annual Dead of Winter event in areas that I have investigated before, I was very excited to hear that in 2017, the event would be held in Carlinville, IL. Not only does this area offer me a location that I haven't investigated before, but it also brought me back to some old memories from High School. How's that for a segue into one of my personal stories? If you want to skip my fun memory, I understand. Although they usually get a laugh, they're not for everyone. So, if you want to skip it, just jump ahead about ten paragraphs.

       When I was a junior in High School, I was greatly involved with my local UCC church. I was also a member of the Fellowship of Christian Athletes at my school. On Martin Luther King weekend in 1994 or 1995, my friend's Matt and Travis, and myself all went to a special church getaway at the Lake Williamson Christian Center in Carlinville. I can't remember if it was through the youth group from church or the FCA, because the three of us were involved in both groups. Of course, this aspect doesn't matter for the story, so moving along.

       Let's be honest here. We were three 17-18-year-old, young stallions. Yes, we were involved in church, but when you have an opportunity to go to an event where there were two girls to every one guy, we weren't just interested in bettering our relationship with the man upstairs. We were also hoping to meet a young lady (as

I am writing this, I am just waiting for lightning to strike around me).

The weekend was great and consisted of lots of fun activities. There was a 3 on 3 basketball tourney that the three of decided to enter. God must have been on my side because I was draining threes like you read about. Not that I'm saying draining threes could be read about in the Bible, although it could have been in there somewhere. We somehow managed to win the tournament even though we weren't the most athletic guys out there.

There was also an evening event where they were going to try to teach the group manners and etiquette. We actually all got paired up with a "date" for the evening that we had to act properly around. The food was great, and the dishware and utensils were probably a little too classy for us. In fact, it didn't take long for my table to begin making music by running our fingers along the crystal glasses full of water, which was totally against the idea of being well mannered in public. It sure did sound beautiful though and it garnered much attention from those around our table.

Unfortunately, the dorms were set up to keep the guys and girls apart after hours. It was pretty much like a prison minus the barbed wire, bad food and fear of dropping the soap. The room that we were in housed about six of us if I remember correctly. Aside from the three of us, there was also a duo named Paul and Jared. One of the six was also a chaperone that was supposed to keep us out of trouble. Our chaperone was a heavyset guy who we dubbed the plumber because you could always see his crack. The first evening we were there, Paul decided to start telling a joke very late at night. The joke lasted about 20 minutes and had absolutely no punch line. Irritated that he kept us awake for that, the logical thing for us to do was to strip him down to his undies.

Then we carried him down the steps and threw him out the front door and into the snow. He kept trying to get back in but we informed him he won't be getting back in until he runs two laps around the building. Needless to say, he didn't tell us any more jokes the rest of our stay.

Since that young man felt that he owed us, we utilized him as a courier our second evening there. Since the other side of our building was where all the ladies were located, we needed to somehow get a message through to them. This was the mid 90's so cell phones were out of the question. We were going to have to get the message to them by delivering it in person, the old-fashioned way. Paul was this guy and he was definitely up for the mission.

We wrote a letter stating that we were hoping to spend some time with some ladies that weekend. We all signed it with our nicknames so we didn't give out our real names. Matt was "Dark Helmet" (Spaceballs reference), Travis was "Gator Man" (he wore a hat that was shaped like an alligator head), I was "Polish Prince" (was Prom Prince in High School and am very much Polish). I think Paul and Jared just signed their real names.

Paul, with letter in hand, darted out the building and ran to the other end where the girls were located. Within minutes he came flying back into our room avoiding any detection and all enemy fire. With the message delivered, we figured by the next day, at the very least we may be sitting near a very special lady. Maybe, if the stars aligned perfectly, we'd even be holding hands.

The next morning, when we all gathered for Morning Prayer, the Pastor stood in front of everyone and said "I'd like to read from a letter that was given to me this morning". With this, we all looked at each other and we knew we were in boat load of trouble. The Pastor also said that when he reads the names at the end of the letter, each person will need to stand up. As the letter was being read, all of our faces were getting very red and it was difficult making eye contact as we stood up when our name was called. Worse part of all, more so than the embarrassment, there was no handholding in the cards for us that weekend. Although there was a final night dance and we were popular there because we actually danced unlike most of the guys that were there.

As far as the letter and how it got into enemy hands. When Paul slid it under the door of one of the rooms, he didn't realize that room's chaperone laid her mattress on the floor right in front of the door. So, when she heard the outside door open, she opened her eyes and saw the light breaking under the door. Then she watched as the note slowly slid underneath the door right under her nose. The girls never even saw it. Cue Little Texas' "What Might've Been" song here. We didn't find love there that weekend, but I remember the events as if they were yesterday!

That flashback was a lot longer than I thought, but I'll get back on course now. Let's develop the story and get into some history about the building that we were able to investigate during the Dead of Winter event.

In the mid 1800's, an idea of building a large courthouse for Macoupin County was heavily influenced by two men. One was County Clerk George Holliday and the other was Judge Thaddeus Loomis. Construction began around 1867 with a modest budget of $50,000. By the time they finished the foundation of the building, a third of the money was already gone. Once they

The front steps of the massive building

completed the cornerstones, all of the allotted money was depleted.

There was a lot of concern over what may have happened to the funds because much of the tax-paying public felt that the funds went far too quickly. Some of these individuals were questioning whether the money they paid was being used to pay for the building or if it was being embezzled by those involved with the construction of the building. If it did all go to the building, perhaps the building was becoming more extravagant than what was originally proposed. Many protests were started by groups of citizens because of these concerns.

By 1869, things were getting worse for the building and the builders. At this point, half a million dollars was spent on the construction. These large numbers only worsened the already brittle public attitudes toward the new courthouse. Public opinion didn't matter though as more and more money was being borrowed to finish the building. Eventually the Illinois government got involved and they passed legislation to use more tax dollars to get the funds needed to complete the building.

Finally, by 1870, the building was completed at a staggering cost of approximately $1,324,000. A far cry from the original $50,000 estimate for completing the building. This is where the nickname, "The Million Dollar Courthouse" comes from.

Of course, with this high cost for the building at the expense of the residents, many red flags were hoisted by the uneasy public. Especially since Judge Loomis had other projects around town that seemed to possibly draw from some of the courthouse funds. One of these projects included a luxurious hotel. Eventually an Anti-Courthouse Committee was formed to look into where the funds were actually dispersed.

After looking into things more closely, Loomis was not charged for any wrongdoings. Holliday, on the other hand, was eventually indicted for fraud, forgery and embezzlement. Due to the charges against him, Holliday disappeared from the area. Nobody knew for sure where he went, but an individual who looked similar to Holliday took up residence in Washington D.C. which caught the eye of some of the informed public. This individual's name was Samuel Hall.

With the resemblance of Hall to Holliday, he was brought back to trial in Macoupin County. Several witnesses were brought in to verify that Hall was indeed Holliday. One witness in particular was the former dentist of Holliday's. Forced to open his mouth as evidence, the dentist was able to show that Hall had the same teeth as well as gold teeth that Holliday had. However, a reverend stepped up to the stand and stated that he couldn't confirm it was Holliday. The court wasn't able to prove that Hall was Holliday, or rather, maybe they didn't want to confirm for fear of them getting called out for any knowledge they may have had towards the movements of funds.

View from the side of the building. That's my car on the left. Just proving I was there to you skeptics.

Hall was released and he immediately went back to his office in D.C. Upon arriving, he packed up his office and was never heard from again. I think the haste with which he used in disappearing removes any doubt that he was indeed Holliday and that he was involved in some crooked activities in Carlinville. This is merely my opinion on the matter though, so it means nothing obviously.

With all the negative energy from these scandalous events, one would have to think there's some ghostly activity hovering inside the building. In some cases, it could just be the negative energy replaying, and in others, I think it's the ghosts of former inhabitants of the building who are still roaming the building. In fact, Judge Loomis himself is considered to be one of the spirits inhabiting the building. He is thought to still preside over the courthouse from his luxurious velvet throne that is still on display today.

The beautiful architecture of the building shows how no expenses were spared with the construction of the courthouse.

This building isn't without its deaths either. Local stories talk about a former employee named Sheriff William Harrison Fishback who was part of a tragic event that occurred in the building. In the 1870's, Sheriff Fishback was found dead in the courthouse one day and unfortunately there are conflicting reports about his status. Some report that he was shot in the back of the head and others report that he was shot elsewhere. Even though some stated the wound was from the back of the head, it was ruled a suicide. One has to wonder if maybe Sheriff Fishback found some incriminating evidence towards the "powers that be" and was knocked off because of it. This of course is all speculation and has no hard evidence to back it up.

Each floor has its own share of activity. In some cases, there is a bit of knowledge as to who is haunting the area, and on others, the encounters aren't tied to one specific individual. On the first floor, there is thought to be the spirit of a little girl who has been seen moving about the hallways. She is said to be one of the former orphans that spent time inside the building. She tends to respond to female guests more than the men though. There have also been encounters with the former Sheriff on this floor. Individuals who spend time in the courtroom on this floor often report that they are feeling queasy and having shortness of breath.

The second floor has an area with several military uniforms on display. These uniforms sometimes give off strange EMF readings. In the main hallway on this floor, there are also EMF spikes that have no explanation as to the source. Some investigators on this floor have seen the name Holliday appear through their various communication devices on several occasions. Maybe it's George Holliday making himself known, or maybe it's a fan of Madonna's song "Holiday" coming through.

On the third floor, in the main courtroom, people have heard voices and footsteps and have even seen dark shadowy figures moving about. A former helper for the Haunted Carlinville Tours even had an encounter with a shadow figure just outside the courtroom. She hasn't been back since.

This of course is just a brief summary of some of the activity that one can expect to hopefully experience inside the Million Dollar Courthouse. Some digging could potentially locate other spirits as well. If you think about the emotion involved in a courtroom, there is no doubt in my mind that some of that emotion can be residual. Harsh verdicts, causing the wrongdoers and their friends and family much grief, could replay itself over and over again. Perhaps an individual who may have been sentenced to death, decided to come back to the place that put that decision on him. The possibilities for sources of the hauntings are endless if one takes the time to divulge in them.

Len Adams and I rode out to Carlinville together for the 2017 Dead of Winter event. Len was speaking at the event and I just planned on setting up a couple tables to sell some of my books and other wares. After the event was over, we intended on staying for the investigation of the courthouse. I had never seen this building in person, and I was completely in awe when we pulled up to it. This building is beautifully designed and is massive. I couldn't wait to get inside.

The interior of the building did not let us down either. The architecture was beautifully done. I am not sure on all the lingo of what is what, I just know whatever style it was, it was incredible. From the huge, heavy doors to the tiled floors, everything was perfect. The doors that lead to the main courtroom even had these antique door knockers on them. Much like the reference to "A Christmas Carol" earlier in the book, I expected to see the door knocker take on the face of Jacob Marley at any point.

The event was great during the day. The speakers were full of knowledge, and I met a lot of new people who came by my table to chat. Several people made my day by telling me how much they enjoy my style of writing. One person was even upset that I wasn't speaking. A reaction like that is very humbling and shows me that there's a first for everything. Once the event was over, we all packed our tables up as quickly as possible. I am not really sure why we were trying to set a record pace because it wasn't necessary. We had plenty of time to kill before the investigation started, so we didn't need to be in a hurry. Once packed up, we all headed out to dinner.

When we returned to the courthouse for the investigation, we found ourselves about 45 minutes early. I was all for that though as it would give me some time to walk around the building and do some preliminary investigating before the rest of the group arrived. Kaylan, the Carlinville Hauntings guide and host for the overnight walked Len and I in through a side door. Immediately upon entering, we were greeted with this massive gust of cold air. Nothing paranormal though. For some reason, the building has this huge vent that kicks on when you open the door and shuts off when the door closes. I am not really sure the purpose of this feature. Len thought maybe it used to be "The Million Dollar Courthouse and Car Wash". The only things I could think is maybe it's to alert security when someone comes in or to dry you off if it was raining outside.

Once in the building, we were on the lower level and we started setting up a staging area for the investigators. As soon as we finished with that, I grabbed my camera and began walking around taking photos of the various areas. After taking about 30 or so photos I came back to my arsenal and grabbed my digital recorder and Ghost Radar and headed to the smaller Courtroom C on the lower level. This is the area where people have had shortness of breath and queasiness. I am not sure why I chose that room other than Kaylan telling me about the effect it has on people. I was willing to take a chance though because something told me to go in there. Any uneasy feelings though would have to be blamed on the ten Buffalo wings I ate the hour before.

I sat in one of the chairs where a lawyer and their client would sit. I turned on the radar and then started recording on the recorder. Unfortunately, Len and Kaylan were just outside the courtroom in the hallway and Len was his usual comic relief. I could hear their muffled voices talking, so I had to be careful not to count them as any potential evidence. With all of the gear ready for use, I began asking some questions. Anytime a word would pop up on the radar I would always repeat it out loud. Even though the recorder would pick up the word being said, it's not always clear during playback, so I try to use this technique every investigation I do.

Several times I had potential interaction with the spirits that were present with me. The first response was when I asked the question, "Do you work here?" This is met with a voice that sounds like a "yes". Shortly after this response, I begin talking about how the spirits could use any of the equipment I have in front of me to communicate with me. As I am stating this, through the Ghost Radar, the word "policeman" pops up. When I heard this, I ask "is there a policeman in here right now? I heard a story about a former sheriff....". At this point I get cut off by the word "hurt" coming through the radar. If I got a chance to finish my sentence, I was going to say something about a former sheriff getting shot. It's very interesting that in a way, my thought was completed before me. There was about thirteen seconds between the two words which was definitely a strange coincidence.

The next bit of activity happened after I asked, "Are you watching over this building?" It sounds like you can hear a soft whistle followed by a whispered "no". Aside from the things projected through the ghost radar, any other responses weren't heard until I got home and listened to the audio closely. That's the tough part of doing EVP if you don't listen to it real time. You don't get the replies until later. Hearing the responses with your own ears at the time the response is made, is something very rare and very special.

With that thought in mind, I was extremely excited, and terrified, when I heard a couple female screams come from behind where I was sitting. They were very soft and distant. I mentioned on the recording that I just heard a woman scream. Then I heard a couple more. All of these were actually recorded on my device. Part of me wants to say that these sounds came from outside. There is a window directly behind me, so perhaps that theory is true. The only problem with that idea is the closest house is almost a block away from where I was sitting. At this point, I can only tell you what I heard and not offer a definitive source of the sound.

A few minutes later I decided to wrap up the session since the people who signed up for the investigation were set to begin arriving. I grabbed my gadgets and began making my way out of the courtroom. When you exit the courtroom, you enter into a little room that connects to the juror's room. If you turn left, you go to that area, if you turn right you enter the hallway. As I popped out of the courtroom and started to turn right, I heard someone walking in front of me in the actual hallway. It sounded like a shuffling sound. I figured it was Len or Kaylan walking past the doorway where I was. When I entered the hallway, Len was still sitting on one of the benches toward the end of the hallway. Kaylan was standing past Len at the very end of the hallway. Whatever caused the sound was definitely not the two of them.

At the discovery of the fact that what I heard couldn't have been them, the hair stood on end and I got the chills. I think my goosebumps even had goosebumps. I walked down to where they were and told them what had happened. Len then stated that when I went up to the other floor with Kaylan, so we could turn lights on and off, he was sitting in the hallway by himself. As he sat there, he kept hearing footsteps coming down the hall towards him. Maybe what I heard was the same person moving down the hall that Len was experiencing earlier.

As people began arriving, we met them all outside in front of the grand staircase that leads to the second-floor doors. Kaylan began telling the tainted history of the building just to get everyone up to speed with the early days of the courthouse. After that we all headed inside, got dried off by the fans, and then she began to provide some investigative equipment to people who didn't have anything to use. She had dowsing rods, EMF detectors, flashlights, ghost radios, etc. After the division of equipment, she divided everyone up into three groups, provided them each with a floor, and set them on their ways. Each group had one hour to investigate their floor, then they would switch. Once each team investigated every floor, we would all meet to go over any possible evidence and then they'd be let go for free roam to go wherever they would like.

The first thing I did was set up my video camera in the courtroom where I had my earlier experience and let it record for a couple hours. Then I left the area and I found myself wandering around quite a bit just to make sure people were enjoying themselves and to answer any questions about investigating that I could. Even though I was visiting the entire building, I kept venturing back to

This is the courtroom where I spent most my time. The seat in between the two tables is where I sat when I was in the room by myself.

the courtroom where the camera was running. All throughout the night I did about three more EVP sessions in that room with various people. Most of these were kind of active and only one was more of a letdown. Here's a breakdown of what happened during those sessions. The first session would be the one from earlier where I was in the room by myself.

Session 2. There were quite a few people in the room with me at this time. Sometimes that makes it difficult because you have to be leery that nobody is making any noises. In fact, there was once instance after reviewing the footage while at home, where someone stated the name "Thomas" appeared on their device. After she states this, I can hear something get whispered on the audio. Luckily shortly after that, I mentioned something about the name Thomas and one of the other people in the room mentioned that they got that name before too. The comment that they made was actually the same exact thing that was whispered. So, from this, I think the person who said the name out loud must have had a friend sitting next to them. That friend then whispered to her that she got that name too which was picked up on the recorder. Then, when I mentioned it out loud, the friend no longer needed to whisper so she repeated herself out loud. Even without the whisper, this means that two different people received the name "Thomas" on their devices. That's the bigger picture here.

During this session, I found myself asking most of the questions. This is fine with me as I know some people are intimidated, or perhaps a bit embarrassed, to ask questions in front of strangers. I asked a question if there was anyone with us right now. Shortly after that, it sounds like a voice saying "help" gets captured on the recorder.

Also during this part of the investigation, I did my faithful knocking pattern trick. When I did it, we didn't hear the two knocks like we should have received. We actually only got one knock. It came from the area where the jurors would sit. The problem is there were a few people sitting and standing in that area. When I asked if anyone made the noise nobody fessed up to it. Although, in a trusting world, that would be good enough, I have to err to caution and think that it could have been somebody that was in the room that made the noise. A little while later I did the same pattern again, which again was met with a definite bang. This time, the person that made the noise admitted to it right away.

I decided to wrap this session up once it started to get quiet and made my way back into the hallway. I wanted to let things settle down for a while before continuing. Maybe I was annoying the spirits and they needed a break from me. I seem to have that effect on people so I am definitely used to it.

Session 3. After mingling with people on the various floors, I headed back down to the courtroom for the next session. There was only one other person in the room with me this time. I ended up setting up a laser grid in the room for this one. The other investigator also put a balloon out with a glow stick in it. This is a neat technique as the light could attract a spirit to it, but also in the dark, you can clearly see if the balloon moves.

I began asking questions and upon reviewing the audio, at one spot on the recorder I picked up a soft female voice. I couldn't really tell what it said at first. Initially, I wondered if it was the other investigator that maybe said something. However, shortly after this voice, the other person, the real person, said something and the voices sounded nothing alike. So, for the time being I thought it could have been paranormal. I wrote this down in my notes as being possibly audible interaction. Later in the session though, the other investigator did say something in response to something I said and it sounded exactly like the other voice. I copied both clips out of the recording and played them back to back, and they were indeed similar. So, I was able to debunk the voice and rule it as being natural.

When we finished with the segment, the other investigator mentioned having chalk so I asked her if she could draw an "X" under the balloon so we could tell if it moved that way as well. Just in case something happened with the camera and it wasn't able to pick up the movement, this would act as a backup plan. Often with my investigations, when all is right, something goes wrong. So, to be able to capture evidence with multiple tools is invaluable.

Just as she approached the balloon, it began to rock back and forth right in front of her. We both saw it act this way. My first thought was she may have kicked it but she said she didn't touch it. My next thought was that maybe her weight on the tiles made the floor move a bit and that made the balloon rock. I had noticed earlier that some of the tiles in that courtroom were loose, so maybe one of those was stepped on before she got to the balloon and that caused the movement. After stepping all around the balloon, we were unable to recreate the motion. As I am writing this, I have only reviewed the audio. Whenever I get a chance to check the video, we'll readdress this.

Session 4. Lots of people were in the room for this one including Len, Kaylan, investigators and a couple girl scouts that were selling cookies to mainly Len and some of the other people at the event earlier that day. I bring up the girl scouts because of something that happened later. The video camera was still running, as was my laser grid. We also used the recorder, several ghost radars and eventually the ghost radio.

The radar was pretty quiet. The only thing that I received that kind of tied to the building was the word "column". The front of the building as well as the large courtroom are both adorned with massive columns. After not getting much action with the Ghost Radar, I decided to break out the Ghost Radio.

Through the radio, we received several potential responses. It was very difficult to figure out what was being said though. I am sure in some cases; we may be making it out to be something it's not. In other cases, most individuals heard the same thing. A couple of which are quite clear. I am not going to say they are clear as day like the paranormal shows say on TV. Most of the times they say "clear as day" it sounds like a jumbled mess off jibber jabber. There I said it! I set ours to FM and had a sweep rate of about 150. I also had it sweeping backwards. Here are some of the highlights of the spirit box session.

One of the questions I asked was if the spirit around us was a former judge. It sounds like a response of "no" was communicated to us. Later we mentioned something about speaking louder so we can hear them better. With this came a "hello" response. It was actually relatively loud and pretty clear. Most people in the room all agreed that it said "hello". I heard hello too, but wanted to make sure other people heard the same thing without me suggesting it.

Later I asked the spirit what their name was. This one is a bit up in the air, but some thought the response said "what's yours?" Later I asked the spirit why they were here and it almost sounds like the word "dead" came through the radio. The last bit of possible evidence was when I asked what the spirits name was a bit later on in the session and we received a response that sounds like "Lauren".

Sometimes the Ghost Radio gets a bit overwhelming with the constant noise. In person, every little pause or voice makes your ears perk up and you start to get really excited. Most of the time it's nothing, but those few and far between moments are what makes it a great tool for investigations.

My favorite event from this session involved the two girl scouts that were in the room with us. After the radio session ended, the two girls decided to leave the room. Within about one minute of them leaving the word "cookies" popped up on the radar. Probably just a coincidence, because I think Cookie is also Kaylan's nickname, but it was pretty funny and fitting.

During the free roam segment, I did manage to scare a group of people. Although I didn't do it on purpose, I did relish in the moment. I always scare my daughter any chance I get, and on a tour, if given an opportunity, I may try to scare the patrons as well. In this instance, I was just walking around seeing if anyone needed any help and to make sure everyone was enjoying themselves. I walked in front of one of the front windows on the second floor to look outside for a moment. This window is right next to the staircases that go between all the floors.

After looking out the window for a moment I turned and started heading up the stairs to the third floor. When I got up there, I heard all this commotion coming from the second floor. There was a group that was visibly shaken by the shadow figure they saw on the wall at the top of the staircase they were walking up. The shadow was there as they started to traipse the staircase, but it quickly vanished. They also mentioned how they didn't see anyone who could have caused the shadow. I was looking over the bannister at them at this point and I was really debating whether not to say it was me.

I decided to let them know because otherwise they may pass off evidence as being truth, that I would know wasn't legit. So, I called down to them and let them know it was me. They didn't hear me so I ran down the steps to them and explained what happened. There was a collective relief that overcame a couple of them, but then there was also a big letdown that it was only me. It turns out that when I stood in front of the window, the street light projected my shadow on the wall at the top of the stairs. They were at the bottom of the stairs and looked up and saw it. I do have to give them credit, although frightened, they did pursue the shadow.

After this event, the evening seemed to be winding down. People were dropping off like crazy. By about 1am, we were down to the last three people. When they finally decided to call it a night, they were very excited to find out that they were the last ones left.

As far as the video footage goes, I didn't get a whole lot of evidence that I would feel is concrete. I think the room must have been pretty dusty because when people moved about, I could see dust moving about. Some of the balls of light could have possibly been spirit energy, but since I saw so much dust, it's hard to offer it as rock solid evidence. I will probably put some of the following clips on my website if I can figure it out just so you can see it. Here are the greatest hits of what I captured.

Earlier I mentioned the whisper that I captured on my recorder. Then I was able to debunk it because the person who whispered it later said the same thing out loud. The video camera actually picked up the same audio and further proved that it was actually an investigator and not a ghost. About twenty minutes into the video I did get two spots with orb movement.

The long hallway on the main floor. Such a beautiful building. I want this tile in my kitchen.

Everyone was sitting still and there was not air circulation in the room.

About forty minutes into the video is where the balloon possibly moved. I watched the clip several times to try and figure out if her foot kicked the balloon or not. It's really hard to tell for sure. I can see that her feet are very close to the balloon; however, I think her feet are already planted when the balloon begins to move. Since there was a glow stick in the balloon, which made the shape a bit awkward so perhaps any movement whatsoever would have been enough for the weight in the balloon to shift. A shift in the glow stick may have created the rocking motion that we noticed on the balloon. I really don't know what to say on this one.

There are several spots with orbs moving about. One time it's going right into Len's head. Other times they are just moving about with no rhyme or reason. On a couple occasions, it looks like there are two attached to each other. It kind of looks like a cell is splitting. I feel like these are most likely dust because of the shape.

Towards the end of the video, there is a group in the room who are trying to get the spirits to make the temperature go down. They were able to monitor the temp with a Mel-Meter and did actually witness a several degrees drop in temperature multiple times.

One thing I'd like to mention after watching my video. If you ever go on an investigation with a group of people, or even a team for the matter, be respectful of those around you. In some cases, there was so much chatter, that it made it difficult to weed out the live from the dead. It contaminates the evidence very quickly.

One other word of advice. If you are investigating with other people and you see a video camera set up in an area, do not stand in front of it for ten minutes. There are several spots on the video where I am adorned with a breathtaking view of a full moon. Keep in mind I was filming inside so I am sure you can figure out what moon I am talking about. I felt like Pee-wee in the original Porky's movie trying to look around it. The problem is, the footage was on a camera and not in shower room. No matter how much I breathed on the viewfinder, it wouldn't move. Yelling at it didn't work like in the movie either. Just sayin'.

With that, this investigation comes to a close. This location is such an amazing building with a troubled past. The investigation was a lot of fun and I met a lot of great people. We may have some possible evidence which is always a plus, but just being in the building made it worth it for me. I could have come up empty on the evidence and I still would have enjoyed myself and recommended it to other investigators. Great location, old friends, new acquaintances all make for a wonderful experience regardless if the building was active for us or not.

A STRANGE INHERITANCE

An acquaintance of mine named Charles inherited a home from his grandmother in South St. Louis, Mo. The home was originally built in 1932 by Charles' great grandpa. The house has been in his family ever since, with the exception of a few years where it was rented out back in the 1950's. When the last renters moved on from the home, Charles' great grandparents moved back in and it's been in the family ever since.

Eventually Charles' grandparents moved into the home. They lived at the location for quite some time. Sadly, in the early 70's the grandfather passed away leaving his wife to take care of the house. She was able to do so for years until her death around 2010. The house was then left to Charles and his family. They have lived in the home ever since.

Although they were very happy to move into the home, they knew there was going to be a lot of work involved. Since his grandmother lived there alone for so many years, and with little income, she was unable to afford some of the necessities needed according to today's living standards. Not only did the house lack some of the modern touches, it also needed a lot of upgrades to the old, out of date structure.

The house stood vacant for about a year before Charles was going to be able to move in. Through the course of that year, they began to slowly work on things to get it up to where they would be comfortable with the living conditions. This included big expenses like replacing the old furnace as well as the duct work. All of this cost a lot of money and took up much of their time, but in the long run, it was going to be well worth the investment.   Not only did it give them a place to raise their family, but it also kept the home in the family.

It is also during this time, with the house being unoccupied, that things began to happen. By things, I mean unexplainable things. One day in particular, Charles was outside of the home when he was approached by one of the neighbors.   The neighbor asked Charles if he could make sure that they turn out the lights in the home when they leave for the day. She also said that the light in one of the side rooms of the house is so bright that it's blinding to them when they see it. It's very bright and even seems to light up the driveway that is right outside the window. These neighbors even live across the street and they are still affected by the bright light. She stated that the lights look like floodlights.

This threw Charles for a loop because there wasn't even any power in the house at this time. There was no way for the light to be left on. When he expressed this to the neighbor, she had a difficult time accepting it as an answer. She just knew that there was power because she had seen the light on numerous occasions. Charles told her that if she sees it again to please call him immediately and he would rush right over to the house.

One evening, on a whim, Charles drove past the house. It was dark out at this time and when he looked towards the house, all was well.   The house was dark, exactly the way it should since there's no power. Around one in the morning, Charles got a phone call from the frantic neighbor. She was very animated saying that the light is on and he needs to come over as soon as possible. Charles drove over to the home as quickly as he could only to find the house completely dark.

The neighbor was waiting outside and when she approached Charles, she mentioned that the light had gone out about a minute before he turned onto the street. Another neighbor that same evening also saw the light on and eventually saw it going out as well. It was hard to deny the fact that this happened since there were two witnesses who gained nothing from their story. Every time Charles would drive past the house at night, he was never able to catch the light being on, although his neighbors continued to do so.

During the time that the house sat empty, several family members would periodically show up to do some cleaning. Charles' uncle came one day and was in the home all by himself. He was working in the dining room closet. Normally this door was always blocked off, and nobody really knew why. I'd like to think this door was blocked to keep "the evil" locked inside. I am sure it was actually blocked to protect grandma's favorite linens. Strangely though, when Charles was a kid, he had an experience in this area. This was long before he had any thoughts that the house may be haunted. He remembers it being an overwhelming sense that someone was watching him from this door. Nobody was there, but he could feel it. When he talked to his grandma about it, she just blew him off and changed the subject. Whether or not she knew it was paranormal or if she truly believed it was his imagination, we will never know.

While his uncle was standing inside the closet rummaging through things, he heard someone say "hey" from directly behind him. He replied with a hello as he stood there waiting for the person to respond. After not hearing an answer, he turned around and found himself completely alone. He looked all over the house thinking that someone must have come in. That's when it hit him that the way "hey" was said to him was exactly the same as his mom used to do when wanting his attention. With that, he ran out the front door, locked it, and then ran straight across the street. He called his wife and had her come pick him up because he wasn't going back into the house. After that event, he refused to go into the home alone ever again.

One evening, the family was all at the house doing some interior work. It was Charles, his wife and their three kids. They were mainly working on removing some of the old paint by chipping it away. They were also beginning to repaint the walls and window settings. The kids at this point were very tired and began getting on each other's nerves. This of course turned into an all-out royal rumble between the kids with no victor and some very irritated parents.

Since they still lived in their old house at this point, Charles decided to take the kids home while his wife continued working at the house. She was on a bit of a roll removing the paint in the kitchen so she didn't want to have to stop. Charles left her alone with intentions of coming back later to pick her up. As his wife moved from area to area of the kitchen, she decided to take pictures of her accomplishments as well as the areas that still needed to be worked on.

We are now going to fast forward a bit to when they finally moved into their new home. Since the "free" home they had inherited became so much of a money pit and drained them of a lot of time and energy, Charles decided he and his wife needed a nice dinner on a special well earned "date night". While they were sitting at the restaurant they began reminiscing about the project they had just completed. She got out her phone to start looking through some of the photos she took inside the house. As she looked through them, she stopped, had a pale look on her face and said something to the extent of, "what the 'blank' is that?" She then passed the phone to

Charles who had a similar reaction as he stared in amazement and terror.

In the photo, you can see Charles' wife (we'll call Diana just for the sake of giving her a name) taking a photo of a window setting. She wanted to photograph what it looked like before she worked on it just so they could document the transformation. This photo was taken after Charles had left to take the kids home for the night. With that in mind, she was in the house by herself. Well, that's what she thought. In the image, you can see her standing there with her camera up in front of her face as she took the photo. This can be seen because of the reflection in the glass.

The odd thing is you can also see the reflection of someone else standing next to her. Actually, not only are they standing next to her, but they are looking right at her. You can see the profile of their face as well as their upper body. The way the figure looks reminds me of an Alfred Hitchcock profile shot. Except I really feel that this person is Native American. The way the brow and forehead looks makes me feel that way. The family had been accused of faking the photo, but I have known Charles for a long time, and he would have no reason to do that. I have no doubt in my mind that this photo is untouched.

The other issue with the image is the location of the photo. With where the reflection is of this individual, they would have to be standing on the sink or stove in order to be reflected in the position they are in. Let's go ahead and mark this down in the "unexplainable" category.

Some of the other activity the family has experienced involves the cookie jars on the kitchen counter. Although the jars are generally kept in a specific order and all facing forward, sometimes they will be relocated or turned around backwards. With three kids in the house, I can't help but think of the "Who Stole the Cookie from the Cookie Jar" song. So maybe the kids got into them and that's why they were out of place. But if you are a kid taking a cookie when you aren't supposed to, wouldn't you try your best to leave everything the way you found it. I know when I was a kid, if I took a cookie, I would make sure to keep all the jars in line so there was no sign of me removing a cookie. I would have worn gloves as well to hide all fingerprints. When I was a kid, my brother had a Nintendo system and he wouldn't let me play it when he wasn't home. He used to coil the controller cable so perfectly around the controller that I was never able to duplicate his technique when I snuck into his room to play. No matter how hard I tried, he always knew when I played it. With this philosophy in place, if stealing a cookie, I doubt the kids would have turned the jars around or put them in a different order as it would bring unwanted attention to the crime scene.

One of the cookie jars did belong to the great grandmother. It's a large one in the shape of a pig. One particular morning, Diana noticed all the cookie jars were turned around. She turned them all back to the correct direction and then left for work. When she got home, they were all turned backwards again. She knew they were all facing the correct direction. It couldn't have been the kids because she would have seen them do it. She then called Charles because she was scared to even be in the house.

Diana wondered if the spirit was possibly his mom or his grandma. To help her decide, she was going to do a test to try and figure it out. She placed a key on the dining room table and said that if the spirit was the grandma, to prove it they would need to move the key across the table. If it was the mother, the key would need to be moved to the floor. When she came back from work that evening, the key was found lying on the floor.

When their son was around two years old, he would often sleep in the same bed as his parents. One evening, the parents were awakened after midnight by their son. He was sitting up in the bed looking towards the corner of the ceiling and the walls. Whatever he was looking at must have been very entertaining because he kept giggling. His giggles were similar to the ones he voiced when he was being tickled. When the son was asked what was going on, he just pointed towards the empty space. At this point, Diana screamed at the corner and said, "Leave my child alone! We are trying to sleep! Go away and let us sleep!" Once she finished yelling at the spirit, the son lay back down and five minutes later he was fast asleep.

Sometimes the family hears banging noises inside the home. The noises are very loud and are heard by all. It almost sounds like, whatever it is, is banging on the furnace. It's so loud that the family thinks it is being hit with a sledgehammer. Usually when the noises start, Charles will just scream at the spirit to knock it off and it usually does. This is a common occurrence though, so it almost needs to be addressed nightly. Usually it would happen between one and two in the morning.

One evening Diana was taking a shower and their youngest son was carrying on about something in the kitchen area. He was screaming bloody murder, so Charles ran in to check on him. His son was standing in the doorway to the kitchen afraid to even enter the room. Charles picked him up and carried him into the kitchen, all the while he was still screaming. It seemed as though his screams were directed at the back door.

Charles decided to set his son down, walk to the back door and open it just to show him there was nothing to be scared of. After proving that nobody was there, his son ran across the kitchen floor, smacked the door with his as hard as he could and screamed "bad". He shook his finger at the door and then ran out of the kitchen and into the bathroom. All Charles could do is stand there in amazement and think "what the hell was that" to himself. His son didn't know a lot of words and he had never heard, or seen him act this way before. When Diana got out of the shower and asked what had happened, Charles told her. It turns out she had a similar experience with the son before.

One of the more terrifying stories in this house also involves their youngest son. When he was only two, Charles had him sitting in his high chair so he could be fed his breakfast. After providing him with a tasty bowl of cereal, Charles made his way into the living room. Moments later, the quiet day was shattered by a blood curdling scream coming from the kitchen. Charles thought that his son may have fallen out of his chair so he stormed in fearing the worse. Thankfully, his son was still upright in his chair, so that was good.

His son was still crying though. When Charles asked him what was wrong, he wasn't able to express himself in words so he just pointed towards the kitchen counter and sink area. There, teetering half on and half off the counter, was his bowl of cereal. It would have been perfect if the cereal was Trix, because that's one heck of a "trick" to have the cereal balancing like that. According to Charles, this was probably the scariest thing he ever encountered in his life. He not only had no way of explaining how the cereal got onto the counter, but he also had no way of explaining how it was balancing without toppling over.

I had hoped to investigate the home at some point, but due to conflicting schedules as well as concerns as to whether an investigation would worsen things, I was never able to conduct one. A few years ago, Charles came into contact with a spiritualist who said they could remove the spirit from the home. Charles was very skeptical about the whole thing, but with the three little ones at the house, he was curious. He met this person at a non- ghost related conference. Without saying too much about his situation, this individual aided by dowsing rods, was able to communicate with the spirit from behind his table. He mentioned things about the haunting that weren't vague but actually dead on with what the family was going through. He didn't say things like "you hear knocking" or "you see a shadow".

One of the more specific things he told Charles was that the reason the spirit bangs on the furnace is because he doesn't like all the new equipment in the house. This was something that does

The photo. See the image of someone standing on the right side of the window?

happen in the house and Charles didn't give out that info up front. He also stated that this was the spirit's ground first and that Charles and his family moved onto the spirit's property.

The spiritualist confronted the spirit during the conference and told him to be gone from the home and to quit being a nuisance. Ever since that event, the house has been relatively quiet. Over the years, there have been a few strange things happen, but nowhere near what it was like before. Charles likes to think that whatever is there, is just watching over the family. He feels anything sinister that was there has moved on and he is ok with coexisting with the way things are now.

To wrap up the tale, I'd like to say a few things about the photo included in this story. Charles has received a lot of ridicule from people over the photo. He has only shown it to friends and family as well as some paranormal investigators. A lot of the people would insist that it's fake and that he photoshopped it or edited it with some other program. Some said it was just a blur or a blemish. Some said it was a real person in the image and that they set it up to fool everyone. All of this has made him very protective of the photo and he hates to even show it to people any longer.

My thoughts on the photo? I definitely do not think it's a blemish or blur. With the detail that is on this individual, you'd have to eliminate that explanation. As far as being a real person in the photo. I would think they would be just as clear as the real person that is in the photo. Looking at the photo closely, they aren't. There's quite a bit of difference between the quality and clarity of the two people.

So, that leaves us with editing the photo. I have encountered this issue a lot in this field. I have people send me questionable photos all the time and you can usually tell right away when the photo is edited. I had a guy on one of my tours show me an image that they swore was real because they took it themselves. The image is of a painting of a woman at a well-known haunted location. In one picture, the woman is smiling and in the other, she is scowling. It looks creepy as all get out, but it's fake. In the scowling photo, you can see where he used a duplicating tool to copy flesh from one part of her face and build it over the area of her mouth. This was done to eliminate her smile.

A zoomed in and enhanced view of the "other" person in the photo.

Unfortunately for the editor, he copied the area near her eyes and because of that; you can see that a portion of her eyebrow mysteriously made its way down to her lips.

Some very poor editing if you ask me. Unless she had a hairy lip, which I guess could be quite possible. She wasn't a very attractive woman.

Charles made it very clear to me that he did not edit the photo. I believe him. It's not like he is putting this photo out there to better himself. The only reason he showed the photo in the first place was to make sure people were seeing what he was seeing. It was more of a way to confirm he wasn't crazy or seeing things. He's not trying to sell the photo. He's not trying to get a television contract. He's not interested in that. So, what would be the use of editing a photo if you aren't interested in the exposure it could potentially bring?

The whole idea of editing paranormal photos drives me crazy. The opinion of whether or not ghosts are real is a longtime battle. Years ago, to get a skeptic to believe, they wanted to be provided a photo. Now that photos are being provided, whether they are real or not, that's not enough. It's not enough because anybody can fake a photo. Where does this leave us with proving that ghosts are real? I wish I knew. I don't think we will ever be able to convince the skeptics because it's their job to not believe. With all the faked photos available to the public, the field has taken a major hit. It's going to be nearly impossible to provide a 100% real ghost photo in the future that sways the opinions of the naysayers because of the amount of fakes available.

Charles made a point to all others that have seen the photo that he doesn't want it put on social media or made commercial. Again, why waste the time creating it if you don't want it seen? Luckily for me, I believe this photo is real, and I am honored that Charles allowed me to put it in my book. It's one of the best ghost photos I have ever seen.

IT WAS A DARK AND WINDY NIGHT

I know I've mentioned the use of the Ghost Radar as a paranormal tool throughout this book. I find myself using it through all the investigations I have done the past few years and I really enjoy it. Here's the issue at hand though. As I've been writing all my stories, I have to wonder if perhaps I rely too heavily on this one tool.

In the future, I will have to be careful with putting too much stock in just one device. I think it's a good complimentary tool and that should be the extent of it. If I use multiple equipment on an investigation and the only form of evidence is captured with just one piece of equipment, it would make me question whether or not the evidence would prove a location to be haunted. With this device, since I find myself trying to make the words correlate to the situation, I can't rely on it solely as being concrete. I need more evidence through multiple devices before I can say for sure that a location may be haunted.

The following story is one that falls into the pit of just not having enough evidence. Although multiple tools were being used, the Ghost Radar was the only one that provided any potential data. With the evidence coming from a singular source, I am not really sure what to think. Here it is for you to decide.

I was contacted by a home owner named Becky. They had purchased a house, built in the 1850's, with the hopes of flipping it to make some money. Although they did a lot of the decorating and smaller tasks themselves, they brought in a carpenter to do a lot of the work that they were unable to do. The house had been worked on for about five months or so before it was finally ready to be put on the market.

When the carpenter met with Becky to do a walkthrough of the house so she could see all the work that was done, he decided to confide in her some startling information. He made it perfectly clear that he was very excited to not have to work in that house any longer. When Becky asked what he meant, he informed her that the house has to be haunted.

He said that while he was working in the house, he kept feeling like he wasn't alone. Not only that, but a lot of his electrical equipment would quit working with no explanation. Other times he would set something down and then leave the room. When he would return, the item would be missing. Then, later in the day, he would find the missing item somewhere in the house where he hadn't been, or where he had already searched before. All of this activity was frightening, but it wasn't enough to make him leave the job early. Now that he was finished with the job, good riddance.

When the family reached out to me to come and check the house out, I was very excited. I had actually metal detected the yard after they purchased the home, so I had some familiarity with it. With it being an older house, I was pretty excited about what we could find. I was a little let down though. Aside from some cool items like old axe heads, one of which appeared hand-made, a military button and a neat dollhouse miniature furniture piece, I really didn't find anything near as old as I would have thought. One of the first items I found was a Chuck E Cheese token. Unfortunately, that piece of history didn't date back to the 1800's.

The investigation was going to consist of myself, Chasidy and the home owner, Becky. We set up a time to go out there one dark and windy night. I am not just setting the story up either; it really was a dark and windy night. The wind was blowing very hard and the sound of it filled the empty house. We had to take that in consideration when we were investigating because any noise could have been caused by the wind.

When we first entered the house, we got the usual tour. The lower level consisted of a front room, small bedroom/office, bathroom and kitchen. Upstairs there were two small rooms, a huge closet and a small bathroom. There was no basement in the home, but they did have a fruit cellar. Access to it was granted by a trap door in the kitchen floor. Naturally I wanted to take a peek at the area so I made my way through the floor and down the rickety ladder. It was probably only about six feet by eight feet in size. You could also access the crawl space from it if you found it necessary. It wasn't creepy as far as a ghostly presence, but my wife would have been absolutely terrified. The cellar was crawling with cave crickets, also known as camelback crickets, camel crickets, or spider crickets. They are also called sprickets or criders, for short. Either way, my wife hates these things, so she would have been scurrying out of that area as quick as possible.

We started the investigation on the first floor of the house. I began pulling some equipment out of my bag and prepping it for use. Becky went around and turned off the lights and fans so they wouldn't interfere with any activity. I set up my video camera in the kitchen aiming over the fruit cellar trap door and towards the staircase. I put my Tri-field meter in the center of the side room. Although we knew the previous carpenter stated he had experiences, he didn't go into detail with what areas may be more active than others. So, with that, we were flying blind.

We began by doing an EVP session utilizing the Ghost Radar and a Digital recorder. At this point I also remembered that I actually had purchased a Ouija board at a local thrift store earlier that day. I thought this would be a great chance to utilize it and see if it works. Chasidy and Becky didn't want anything to do with it though, so it stayed in the car, calling to me…. softly.

We were asking a lot of questions as to who may have been tormenting the carpenter, but we weren't getting much luck. At one point, I did get what sounded like a deep breath being taken. I don't believe it was one of us doing it because I would have made mention of it on the recording when it happened. This session was about fifteen minutes long and this was the only thing of question that occurred on the recording.

When we started the next session at one point on the recording it sounds like a cough was caught on audio. Again, there were three of us in there and there were gale force winds outside, so it may have been something explainable. On the radar during this session, we did get the word "slope". Here's where we start trying way too hard to make things make sense. The first though was that when I was metal detecting the yard, there was a big slope to it. When the house was getting worked on, they leveled all the ground out which got rid of the slope. Could the spirit have been talking about the slope of the yard? I think it was a random word that we were able to grab hold of even though it may not have had anything paranormal to it.

The name "David" also came through the radar during this time. It was one of the only names we had the entire night of investigating. When a name comes up, all of a sudden, all focus is on the fact that that must be the name of the spirit haunting the house. This of course was decided with no historical research to prove the point. We tried to communicate with David, but the only response we got was on the radar. The word "stronger" came up.

In an attempt to get some kind of activity, I spoke to the spirits and told them that they can use energy from the surroundings of the house. They can pull energy from the air, or from me, or from the devices we have around the house. I explained that I understand that it's difficult and it takes a lot of energy to communicate with us. At this point, there's a noise that comes from another room. Again, could it be the wind?

At this point I tried to do the knocking pattern trick. Which, you may have noticed after reading this book, I like to use that method. Although I didn't hear a response of a knock somewhere in the house, we did hear something else. When using the Ghost Radar, if you have the volume up, it makes a loud tick noise when an energy source pops up on the radar. After I did the knocking pattern and am waiting for the two knocks, you can hear two ticks come from the radar. Again, I'm thinking it was just a coincidence, but it was timed quite well.

The only other radar evidence we captured on the first floor of note are as follows. I wanted to try and see if I put something down in a room, would it disappear like the carpenter's tools did. So, I took a flashlight and put it in the side room alongside the Tri-Field Meter. When I walked into the room there was a bit of a temperature drop that was definitely noticeable. While I was in the room, the word "captured" came through the radar from the other room. Of course, my justification for this word popping up is when I went into the room; I must have caught the spirit in there.

While we were trying to communicate further with the spirit, the word "afraid" popped up. We ran with this a bit. We started to ask the spirit if he was afraid of us and we reiterated that we weren't there to hurt him. Then the word "friendly" came up. We asked if the spirit was now communicating with us and the response was "couldn't". Shortly after that the word "sitting" came up which we then asked if the spirit was sitting with us. I should note that two of us were sitting on the floor at this time. We asked if the spirit where it was sitting by us and the word "nervous" came up. Maybe these were truly responses to some of the questions we asked or perhaps just emotional cries as to what the spirit was going through. I really can't say for sure.

The only other significant response that I found relevant was when I addressed if the items I found metal detecting in the yard belonged to the spirit we were communicating with. I mentioned finding two hatchets and I asked if they were his. The word "made" came up which was interesting since I think one of the hatchets may have been hand made.

After feeling the lower level of the house was quiet, we decided to make our way upstairs. We kept the flashlight and Tri-Field meter in the lower level side room. I took my full spectrum camera, digital recorder, ghost radar and ghost radio up with us. Becky and Chasidy went into the far room, and I stayed in the room at the top of the stairs. I set my recorder in the doorway that divided the two rooms. Then we began to ask questions.

At this point, Becky, who had been warm the whole evening, started to get very cold. She was actually shivering because of it. We began to kind of think about things that we encountered all throughout the investigation at this time. There wasn't a whole lot of activity other than a couple noises and some temperature drops. It seemed that most of the evidence was still centered around the radar. As we began to think about some of the words that came through, there seemed to be a common theme.

Keep in mind the home was built in the 1850's. Some words of note were union, gray, captured, and disease. We started to play an angle of perhaps the spirit is tied to the Civil War. As we began addressing that theory, the first word that came up was "shot". Again, this could all be coincidence, but it was interesting.

After this, the room got quiet for a bit. I did start using the Ghost Radio to try and stir some stuff up, but there wasn't any concrete interaction with it. We didn't use it for very long when we decided to turn it off. The radar seemed to slow down for a bit, but at one point the word "talmage" came up. I had never even heard that word before and definitely had never seen it come through a device. That's when Becky said it may be a last name. I coupled it with David and did a search of David Talmage on my phone. Now, I want to make sure you realize I am not saying that this is who is haunting the house. But, when I did a search of that name, I found a person with the same name who lived in a completely different state. The weird part of it though is the anniversary of his death was the exact night of our investigation, March 6th. Weird, but most likely it is just a coincidence.

A couple other odd things happened came shortly before we wrapped up the investigation. We were still upstairs when the name "Cade" came over the radar. This was interesting because earlier that day, Becky's grandson Cade came over to see the house. Not too long after his name came up, the word "airplane" came through. When Cade was at the house, he was holding his favorite toy airplane in his hand during the visit. Another strange coincidence?

Before we decided to wrap it up, I started to get some chest pains. It felt like heartburn but a bit different. It was in the right spot in my chest for heartburn, but it felt like something on the outside was causing it. I know that sounds weird, but it's the best way I can describe it. I didn't say anything about it to anyone because I figured it was caused by something I ate. While I was suffering through the pain, the word "pressure" came up which was very similar to the feeling that I was getting? It did feel like something was applying pressure to my chest and causing the pain.

Although at this point I mentioned to the group that it's pretty quiet, so let's go ahead wrap it up, I really meant, someone is hurting me, I can't take it, I want to go home.   I was really hoping that when we went downstairs, the flashlight would have been gone. We kept telling the spirit that while we were upstairs, it would be the perfect time to hide the flashlight on us. Unfortunately, it was in the same spot I left it so he didn't take our advice.

So, with that, I gathered up all my belongings, and we said farewell to the house. The next step would be to go home and review all the audio as well as the video and see if there's anything else I may have captured that would give us another source of evidence. After checking all the audio, there really wasn't anything substantial except for the few things I mentioned with possible noises.   That leaves only the video. With the video, I fell asleep watching it. It was very uneventful. You can hear the couple sounds that we heard with our own ears, but you can also hear all the wind blowing outside. So I can't really use it as evidence of ghosts, it can only be offered as evidence of a dark and windy night.

I really liked the house but I can't say for sure that it's haunted. Having all potential evidence only coming from one source really makes it difficult to prove it one way or the other. I think with future investigations I really need to shy away from relying on just one device and use my complete arsenal. After all, it's going to take a lot more than a $1.99 app to persuade the skeptics. It can be part of the persuasion of course, but not all of it.

DUELING PHANTOMS

When I began working on the new book, I found it hard to find some new locations that readers of the paranormal have never read about before. I love writing about residences, because they usually aren't publicly available. The bad side about writing about homes is the fear that some rogue investigators may go banging on the individual's door to see if they can come in, track dirt all over the house, duct tape wires down to the original hard wood floors, raid the fridge (don't even act like I am the only investigator who has done that), etc. etc. So, with the specific location story that is in the pages to follow, I do want you readers to fight the urge to go to this location. I don't want to bother the current home owners with paranormal team after paranormal team requesting permission to investigate. In some cases, think of a paranormal team as a vampire, you have to be invited in before you can step into the home.

Several years ago, I met an individual named Brian Gray. He was in the process of starting his own ghost tour in Southern Missouri. We talked for quite a bit as he had quite a few questions about things. Later, he even came on one of the tours I was leading just to see how I led them. We've stayed in touch through the years and since I knew he had a bunch of great stories from the Ste. Genevieve area, I drilled his brain to collaborate on a story with me. So first off, as most of you are used to my stories, it's only natural that Brian should start off in a similar way. He starts with a story of his own and also gives you a backstory on how he got into the paranormal. After that we'll delve into one of the most haunted locations that he highlighted on his tour. I couldn't let Brian write everything though, so among some editing, I am also chiming in on his story. So, there, deal with it. From here on, the story is Brian's except for where you see my name in parentheses.

HOW IT ALL BEGAN

We all hear stories about things that go bump in the night. The light that was on even though you swear you turned them all off, or the heavy footsteps you heard in the hallway when you were alone in the house. These are just a few of the things that have us dreading what may linger in the darkness. Often times, little things like this can be explained. In most cases, it could even be replicated if one was so inclined to try. After you explain things naturally, sometimes you are left with the ones you can't explain. The stories that cannot be explained are what keep us trudging along in this field.

As a tour guide and former owner of a ghost tour company, I can tell you that there were many times when I really had to question what it was that I witnessed. I call myself a skeptical believer if that makes any sense. I feel as if I walk a narrow line between what is reality and what is just a figment of my own imagination. As I would so often say during the beginning of my ghost tour, you didn't come here to hear about me, did you? You came to hear about ghosts. So that is where I will begin.

It was a dark and stormy night! Ok, it really wasn't. Truthfully, it was a hot sunny afternoon in the little town of Summit, AR. I was seven years old, and I lived on an old dusty road just outside of town. Summit wasn't very big then, and it hasn't changed much since I lived there. The population at the time was only a few hundred, but of course that was quite some time ago. It was a mile walk every day from my house to the end of the road where I had to catch the bus, and it was uphill both ways. (*Luke – I really did walk uphill both ways. It was usually snowing, or at the very least, hurricane like* conditions in the Midwest. *Those Midwest hurricanes aren't something to mess with.*) I'm kidding about the last part of course, but it was a dusty road with overgrowth and trees on both sides. Along the road was a really big hill that I just hated to walk up. All the kids that lived on my road hated that hill, and we had a friend who lived at the very top. In order to bypass the hill, we decided to make a trail that cut through the woods. It was so much easier than taking the exhausting hike up a red clay mountain with boulders the size of Texas in the middle of it.

One day I decided to head up to my friend's house to hang out. Because of this, I had to leave the safety and comfort of my little house on the prairie and make my way up the long, winding road. (*Luke - Cue the Beatles song.*) This is where the story gets interesting. I guess before I go any further, I want to tell in all seriousness that what I am going to describe to you is absolutely accurate and was in no way, my imagination. The entrance to the trail was narrow, and cut through a small opening in a barbed wire fence. We had used gardening tools to cut away the brush and after making many passes through the woods, we wore a visible trail in the dirt. (*Luke – Damn vandals. I wondered who damaged my fence.*) It wasn't very far to the other side, and when I stood at the entrance, I could see the house a short distance away. Lost in thought, I turned to the left to begin walking up the trail, and that is when I saw them.

Moving from right to left, I saw the apparition of a young boy. He looked like he might have been ten years old or so. He was wearing overalls with the usual fashionable white t-shirt on underneath them. I do not recall seeing any feet, just his body from the knees up. (*Luke – I always found this interesting. The theory behind why you may not see the feet is this. If the*

haunting is a residual haunting where the spirit is
replaying what he did in life, then maybe he walked that
same path over and over again. With the changing of the
grounds, perhaps when he walked it in life, the ground
was lower than it was when Brian encountered him. So,
if the ground was lower like it originally was, we would
see his feet. It's not that they aren't there, they are just
concealed by the changing earth.) This little boy seemed
to have come out of nowhere. It was almost as if he was
running through the woods and he just happened to see
me. He stopped, and turned towards me looking directly
at me.

Then almost immediately after the boy appeared,
the apparition of a young girl around a similar age came
from the same direction. She was wearing a dress and I
could see that she had long hair. She was running as
well, and when she approached the boy, she stopped as
he did and looked right at me. I could see completely
through both of them, but they were solid enough that I
could see all the features of their faces. All of this took
place in a matter of seconds, and I was completely frozen
in fear. Then it happened…as I was standing there with
two spirits staring me down, the girl laughed!! (*Luke –*
Why are ghost kids laughing so terrifying? I'd prefer to
have some disfigured spirit approach me with an axe than
a ghost child smiling and laughing in my general
direction.) Every hair on my head stood straight up! I
heard her laugh out loud! I started screaming and
running as fast as I could back home. I was carrying a
backpack which I just threw down as I was running away.
I remember not stopping and definitely not looking back
for fear that they might be following me.

I burst through the front door of my house yelling
about seeing two ghosts. My mom didn't know what was
wrong and thought that I was hurt. It took her a long
time to get me calmed down enough so I could tell her

what happened. I was so afraid that I had her go back and get my backpack for me. (*Luke – Always send someone else when you are too scared to go into an area. I am sure it was easy for his mom to find the backpack. She just had to follow the trail of pee.*) For the rest of the time that I lived down that road, I never took that trail again, and I would always walk on the opposite side of the road (*Luke – Don't forget, uphill both ways*). Most of the time I would put my head down and run past the entrance to the trail. It was very real, and I get goosebumps just thinking about it. Whether you are a believer or not, when someone asks me if I have ever seen a ghost, I can tell them without a shadow of a doubt, that yes...I have seen a ghost. (*Luke – Ummm, two ghosts actually.*)

I have heard when you are a child, your mind is open and this allows some children to see things that are beyond belief. I guess that day, it was my turn. (*Luke – This is something I totally agree with. I have mentioned this theory before in my previous books. I think as adults, our minds only let in what they can comprehend, or explain.   When there are things that our mind doesn't understand, the door goes up and they aren't allowed in. Since kids' brains aren't as developed, perhaps things slip through that normally wouldn't. This is just a theory, but it sure sounds like I know what I am talking about. I am not a doctor, but I'll play one for this book.*)

FENWICK HOUSE

Ste. Genevieve was established around 1735 making it the oldest settlement in the state of Missouri. Because of this, it is also home to the oldest cemetery in the state. One of the most unfortunate tragedies in Ste. Genevieve's history happened to the gentleman who lived in what is now known as the Fenwick House. His name was Dr. Walter Fenwick. In 1811, there was a duel fought between Thomas Crittenden and Doctor Fenwick. Both of them were well respected residents of Ste. Genevieve. Crittenden was a lawyer and brother of Senator Crittenden of Kentucky. Dr. Fenwick was the town's only physician, and a polished gentleman. Both were very popular and regarded by the community as brave and gallant men. The cause which led to the fatal encounter was one with which Dr. Fenwick originally had nothing to do with. He was drawn into the quarrel by a chivalric devotion to and regard for his brother, Ezekiel Fenwick. Ezekiel owed money to Thomas Crittenden allegedly over a gambling debt. Ezekiel did not pay, and instead issued a challenge to Mr. Crittenden. Mr. Crittenden did not accept on the grounds that Ezekiel was a thief and therefore not a gentleman. In defense of his brother, Dr. Fenwick fought the duel on Ezekiel's behalf.

They met October 1st, 1811 on Moreau's island, located just outside of town on the river. (*Luke – I find it interesting that a lot of duels were fought on islands which were situated in waters between two states. Most likely, this was done to protect them from any state sanctions against duels. Islands were usually free of local law enforcement due to neither state claiming the ground.*) Gen. Henry Dodge was on hand for the duel. As the duel commenced, Dr. Fenwick fell mortally wounded, and expired a short time afterwards. Mr. Crittenden left the duel unhurt. Dr. Fenwick is buried, across the street from his beautiful home, in Ste. Genevieve Memorial Cemetery. He is actually buried at an angle so that he faces his house. This is the only tomb in the cemetery that is not straight. (*Luke – Maybe his brothers grave plot should have been the crooked one...see what I did there? Thief, criminal, crooked. Too soon? Never mind.*)

This wasn't the only tragic event that occurred with Dr. Fenwick. He also had a young son named Zenon who died at a very young age. It is believed that he passed at 9 years of age, but they did not keep very good records at that time and his stone is difficult to read. Both Dr. Fenwick and his son Zenon are buried together in the cemetery. Even though their bodies are still at rest in the cemetery to this day, both Dr. Fenwick and Zenon are still very active in the Fenwick House.

Many stories could be told about the Fenwick House, and believe me, there are quite a few interesting ones. There are probably enough to fill a book if one were so inclined. For our purposes though, we are just going to stick to a few of my favorites. The few I am going to tell you though were told directly to me from the owners of the home or are my own personal experiences.

When the current residents moved in, they had the man from the electric company come out to start new service. Every time new service was started on the building, a tag would be put on the box. One day the new owner noticed there were quite a few service tags on his box so he went to investigate why that would happen. The span of time between each tag was a bit strange. One month, two months, six months... it seemed as though no one stayed in the home for very long. Disturbed by this finding, he called the landlord to find out why tenants don't seem to stay very long. The landlord then informed him that his house was haunted, and that is why no one stayed there for any length of time. Not intimidated by the story, the family decided to stay at the home anyway. Because of their lengthy stay in the home, there is no shortage of their paranormal experiences inside the dwelling.

Originally, this home was only two main rooms plus the attic where Zenon was believed to stay. Sometimes a ball is heard bouncing and rolling across the attic floor followed by the running of a child. Then the ball bounces back to the other side, followed by the same footsteps. Back and forth, back and forth as if someone is playing ball on the attic floor. (*Luke – Goonies reference! Follow those size 5's!)* Here is what makes this story truly unique. Years ago, the attic floor was removed leaving only the bare rafters.   Then, in between the rafters, the space was filled with insulation. With that in mind, Zenon is interacting with an environment that is no longer there.   There's no attic floor to run across any longer.

One night, when the wife got home in the evening, she found that all the lights were off in the home. As she entered the house, she heard a noise coming from the kitchen area. She thought it was her husband, so she called out to him.   After not receiving a response, she walked towards the kitchen with her lighter to see if the noise she heard was him. As she approached the kitchen, she saw a young boy peek around the corner and look directly at her. His head was a little below the counter top which probably puts him at around four feet tall. The boy then moved his head out of sight and when she investigated the area, there was nobody there.

Along with the kitchen and the attic, there are several other experiences they have had with Zenon. When the family is sleeping, if their feet are uncovered, he will start to play with their feet. (*Luke – Sounds like a bit of a foot fetish.)* Sometimes the family has heard a childlike voice calling out "Papa", and reciting the words "come see me". The little boy also likes to play with the toys on the front table by the door.   The family has actually discovered a way to calm things down when the boy gets too active. If they place candy in a bowl for him, that will appease him and he will stop causing trouble for a while. (*Luke – This is the exact opposite of my house. When my kids get candy, they run around like crazy, they break bottles and start bar fights; they vandalize the city and take part in other comic mischief. That's just what one M&M causes. We have to keep the hard stuff like Peanut Butter Cups locked away for their own good.)*

Zenon is very active in the home, and from what I understand, he has taken a liking to the current homeowners. One day, the owner was taking a walk outside, as he does most days, and he noticed people smiling at him as he made his way down the street. He politely smiled back, but thought it was a bit odd. Especially since the people passing by kept looking down and smiling. They weren't even making eye contact with him. He kept walking, and took a break on some steps just a few blocks from his home. He noticed two women approaching him, but instead of saying hello to him, they looked down and said "Are you taking a walk with your grandpa?" Completely stunned he looked up at them and asked "Who are you talking to? I am the only one here!" The two women in a panic straightened up and quickly took off down the street proclaiming that he was crazy. Apparently, spirits need to get out of the house sometimes as well!

Of course, not everything encountered here is friendly. In the home, there is a small closet in one of the bedrooms. (*Luke – I hate little closets. I attribute it to the fact that they conceal little secrets. Or maybe even little creatures.)* This closet is believed by the owner to be the entrance to the attic where Zenon stayed. It would have been the entry way with a ladder going up through the opening. They say that you can see where it was boarded up after they filled the attic with insulation. One night the owner was sleeping and he heard a noise coming from the closet. The door was shut, so he didn't pay too much attention and went back to sleep. He then heard something even louder banging around from the tiny space. What happened next was one of the only times that he was truly frightened in the home.

He saw a light shining from inside the closet, a closet that has no light fixture of any kind. He jumped up and ran to closet to open it and see what was inside, but he was unable to! The door was being held shut from the inside by something more powerful than he was. (*Luke – Obviously, the ghost wanted his privacy, and who are we to deny him that!*) He felt a bone chilling cold in the room that went right to his core. Then as quickly as the cold arrived, it went away and the door was able to be opened. You have to be careful, and be prepared. You never really know what you are up against, or what is on the other side of the door.

Not too long ago a group of paranormal investigators came to the home for an investigation. During their time inside the home, they were able to validate that Zenon was still at the location. The investigators asked who was in the home with them and a voice comes through and says the name "Zenon". I even heard the EVP and you can clearly hear the name Zenon being uttered. That wasn't the most interesting thing that happened that night though. Actually, it was far from it.

After many attempts, one investigator was not getting the response that he was looking for from Dr. Fenwick. He decided to go out to the front porch of the home and said "Come on Dr. Fenwick, if you don't do something I am going to shove my boot up your ass!" A few minutes later, the investigator came back into the home stumbling and acting funny. (*Luke – Perhaps he was the one who had a boot stuck somewhere.*) He asked if he could use the bathroom because he wasn't feeling very well. After he walked around the corner towards the restroom, everyone heard a loud thump. When they ran after the investigator, they found he had passed out cold and hit his head on the bedpost on his way to the bathroom. After waking up and being told what happened, he stated that nothing like that had ever happened to him before. That goes to show that if you are going to use provocation, you better be prepared for what may happen. (*Luke – I am a huge advocate of not provoking spirits to do things. It's all about respect. It's also about safety. If you provoke someone in life, you can at least prepare yourself for how they may react to it. When you can't see what you are provoking, how can you defend yourself from their reaction?*)

MY FENWICK HOUSE INVESTIGATIVE EXPERIENCES

Having been on quite a few investigations, I have to say that what I experienced in this tiny historic home has to be the most frightening out of all of them. My team and I arrived around 9:45 PM and began to set up our equipment. We of course had Mel Meters, EVP recorders, spirit boxes and all the other paranormal gear that you would see during a routine investigation. Definitely not like the ones you see on the TV though. After setting up our equipment, we turned off all the lights and began with a couple twenty-minute EVP sessions. Call and response seemed to work very well inside the home. After reviewing our sessions, we had captured several great EVP's including one telling us who we were communicating with. We then decided to get out the spirit box for one of the EVP sessions. It didn't take long before we started to get some interesting vocalizations coming through the device. After about an hour, everything began to slow down. Since nothing else was coming through, we decided to take a break and wait until closer to midnight to commence. Coffee and caffeinated beverages were scattered around the room, and we passed the time by talking about the home's history and the experiences that the owners had in the home. (*Luke*

– Some of my best experiences happen during caffeine induced states with friends around midnight.)

Finally, midnight was upon us, and we were told that a lot of activity happened towards the back of the home. We decided to change focus, so we packed up our gear and moved to a tiny room in the back of the house. It wasn't very big, but was large enough for a few people to fit in with some equipment. Once again, we turned off the lights and began our session. This time though, things just seemed to be a bit different. The air felt thick and heavy, and there was a general feeling of uneasiness in the room. My associate and I did a quick EVP session, but after only a few uneventful minutes, we moved on to the spirit box. Now I don't know how you feel about using a spirit box, but it can be a great tool for communication. Just know what you're getting into before you take that step.

We were getting voices through the spirit box almost immediately, and we really felt like things were going very well. Then, something happened, and to this day, I cannot explain it. It suddenly became very cold. The room felt as if someone opened the door during a cold winter night and left it open. The spirit box was running but no voices were coming through at this time. Whatever was physically in the room with us though, had decided to make its presence known in another way. My associate was sitting across from me on a small set of stairs that led up to the kitchen. Behind him, about 20 feet, was the front door that led out into the street. There was a really bright street light that was shining through the glass in the front door lighting up the living room and the kitchen area as well. I could even see some of the light shining on his back as he sat on the stairs. We all noticed how cold the room had become and started talking amongst ourselves when it started to become dark…very dark. I don't really know how to describe what happened next. When someone asks me what we saw, the best way for me to describe it is like this. I tell them that it looked like something or someone was moving in front of the light and choking it all out. It was almost like a black cloud blocking out all signs of the sun. The light from the outside street lamp was all but gone as if something was moving through the kitchen and putting up a massive black curtain. (*Luke – I've encountered situations like these as well. It's very hard to describe what happened to people unless they actually experience it along with you, or perhaps they have experienced it before.*)

In that moment, I was truly afraid and I remember thinking to myself, what have I got myself into? Everyone else in the room noticed the darkness as well, and we started to quickly realize that clearly, something was in the room with us. The next words I spoke may sound cliché, but I didn't know what else to say. I said, "Something is here with us." (*Luke – You think, Captain Obvious?*) In that moment, we made the decision to stop the session and the lights were turned on. We closed out the spirit box session, gathered all of our equipment, and wrapped up the investigation for the night. The feeling was like nothing I have ever felt before, and have not felt since. It actually had a physical effect on my associate, and he felt ill after the investigation. We returned to the shop where we hosted the ghost tours and burned some sage just in case anything decided to follow us home. (*Luke – It's funny how when stuff starts getting good, sometimes we get out. Totally defeats the purpose of what we do, but it goes to show, we all get scared when it comes to the unknown.*)

MY FAVORITE STORIES TO TELL ON THE TOUR!

Let's start in the basement, I mean isn't that where a lot of spooky start anyway? (*Luke – True dat! Not just limited to the basements either. Any little hidden away area, crevice, crawl space, etc., all seem to have something residing in it just waiting for the opportunity to shanghai an unsuspecting victim*). It doesn't even have to be a creepy old basement filled with antiques that have been collected from haunted houses and insane asylums either. The basement of the home is from what I can imagine, what most historic homes basements are like. A structure built above a giant hole dug into the earth. This home in particular has had some concrete poured on the floor so that the occupying family could make some usable space out of it. I am sure having washers, dryers and hot water heaters resting on floors of dirt and stone wouldn't be ideal. So, needless to say, some renovation has been done to a portion of the basement. However, the rest of the basement is just dirt walls hiding all kinds of secrets.

The basement stories started with whispers heard below the home, in the dark corners where you couldn't see. That's all it was at first, just noises or something that resembled a voice. (*Luke – I hear these whispers all the time. They tell me to do things. Bad things. Usually I don't listen to them. Sometimes though, sometimes I do*). Over time the whispers grew louder and started to become much more audible. The family knew what they heard, and could not believe it. In an effort to do some investigating, they started to dig out the dirt that was in the basement. They found everything from old medicine bottles, to an antique mortar and pestle.

One of the more interesting finds was a piece to an old Winchester rifle hidden in the rafters. Someone had taken the time to cover the rifle piece with some type of mud or plaster. I assume this was done to keep it concealed. Why would you need to keep a piece like that hidden away though? Your guess is as good as mine, but bringing it out into the light, brought something else out as well. The owners were kind enough to let me borrow the piece for a few days just so I could do a little research on the relic. I was able to find the serial number, but unfortunately there was a fire at the rifle company a long time ago and a lot of the paperwork containing information about particular guns was lost forever. Due to that, I wasn't able to properly track the serial number down.

I was told that I shouldn't bring the rifle piece to my home, but I decided to do so anyway. Even with it being against my better judgement. (*Luke – That's just what guys do. Or to quote a professional football player, "He just does what he do."*) Deciding to keep the gun piece in my house provided us with a very interesting three days to say the least.

The first night that I had the piece in my home, I was at work. My wife called me concerned because the lights were flickering on and off inside the house. She told me that the lights had been doing that all evening, and she was just going to go to bed. She shut off all the lights in the house and walked into the bedroom. Thirsty, she turned around to go back into the kitchen to get a drink of water. The lights were all turned back on even though she had just shut them off moments ago.

The next night I was at home by myself, and I brought the piece into the bedroom and placed it on the nightstand. I wish I was exaggerating when I tell you this but I am not. I climbed into bed and all of a sudden, the bed started to rapidly shake. (*Luke – Come on Brian, what were you up to?*) Not up and down, oh no...side to side! I jumped off the bed and immediately looked at the rifle fragment still sitting on the table. I moved it into the other room and didn't have any other problems the rest of the night.

It was however night three that made me get the piece out of my home for good. I was once again at work and my wife was home alone. She was watching television when someone walked in front of the window to our house and just at that moment the television remote flew off the table from the center of the room! She called me in a panic, and let's just say that I returned the piece to the owners and blessed our house the very next day. They say that spirits can attach themselves to items. If that is true, this particular relic had something hanging onto it pretty tight. (*Luke – Still really curious about why it was in the rafters. It had to be for concealing purposes. I have a feeling that gun has a very dark past.*)

There is also a story of a gentleman that was hanged from the hanging tree in Ste. Genevieve. This man was sentenced to death and he was dispatched from this tree that is resting on the side of a large hill located at in town. His name was Peter Johnson and he was convicted for committing murder. He was actually the first person to be hanged in Ste. Genevieve. A public hanging was a big ordeal, and the whole town would come out to witness this event on August 3, 1810. As if being hanged wasn't bad enough, the body was then sent to the good doctor for "scientific research". Rumor has it that the body may have been buried somewhere close to the home or maybe possibly even in the soft dirt below the house. (*Luke – Wait, you mean the basement? The plot thickens.*)

Soooo, how about those whispers that are heard in the basement? I used to love to tell this story in the basement during the tour. It was always interesting to see the big men standing up front and by the doorway. Often times they would put their wives or partners behind them so their backs could hug the dark cold air and protect the big man from what lurks in the darkness. I would then tell them that from the very spot they were standing, a voice would whisper "Doctor, Doctor." (*Luke – Great Thompson Twins song!!*) These stories of course were told to me by people who experienced them, so I am passing them along to you. Was all of this just one big coincidence? I will leave that to you to decide for yourself.

Sometimes sleepy little towns can have the most activity, and be the most haunted, especially historic towns with a past. These incredible windows to the past are bound to have some haunted history and secrets that are just waiting to be discovered. Some may call it investigating, or ghost hunting, and some may call it an adventure. However, it isn't the name that is important, it is the experience. In all the time that I spent in dark basements, abandoned buildings, and dusty attics it was always about the experience for me. Being in the moment and taking part of something greater than myself. I leave you with this though. No matter what you do, be safe and be smart. Oh, and don't forget to tip the author! (*Luke – Well said! I'd also like to add that it's about the company you bring with you. I've met a lot of great people since I've been investigating. If you don't surround yourself with good people, investigating loses its appeal pretty quickly.*)

THE MINERAL CURE

When I first started getting into ghost investigating, back when my hero Troy Taylor nurtured me and took me under his wing, the Alton Hauntings tours did a lot with the Mineral Springs Hotel in Alton, IL. As years passed, the building went in a different direction, and our tours no longer entered its once welcoming doors. As of 2016, the sky opened up and we were once again able to traverse the darkened halls of this incredibly haunted building. Although I wrote about this building in my first book, and it's been covered in numerous other books and videos, I am going to rehash some of the history and of course go into great detail about the recent investigation I did there.

The Mineral Springs Hotel wasn't even in the plans of the Luer Brothers originally. The two brothers had a meat packing plant in Alton, and they intended on building an ice plant around 1909. These plans were quickly discarded after early construction of the grounds revealed mineral water to be present. As the water was tested, it appeared to be highly mineralized and suggestions were made to the brothers to cancel the ice plant idea and build a spa instead. The brothers went from building a much-needed ice plant to building a large, massive hotel and spa.

Although the original business focus may have changed, the brothers were very excited about the new business venture. Construction of the hotel began in 1913 and opened less than a year later in 1914. Much fanfare accompanied this hotel and the services rendered. The whole idea of mineral water was a national craze at that time. I think what heightened the craze was that the medical world was backing the medicinal qualities that mineral water had to offer. It was thought to be the cure all, end all of all diseases. It didn't matter what ailed you. Anything from smallpox to an in-grown toenail, mineral water would cure you. Of course, I am exaggerating, but it was definitely a money maker for the two brothers to play off of this medical fad.

The mineral water wasn't the only draw to the building however. It was a beautiful building that boasted several other amenities. It had one of the largest swimming pools in the state of Illinois. To look at this pool by today's standards, it's actually not all that exciting. The pool was located in one of the many sublevels of the building. Underneath that level, there was a second swimming pool. This pool was only used by men because swimsuits were optional in that one. Hard telling what kind of extra minerals were pouring out of various orifices into that water. Not my cup of tea when it comes to enjoying a refreshing swim.

The hotel also had a bar, a cigar shop and a bottling plant that shipped bottled mineral water out of the area via the railroads. In the early days, the hotel would move a modest amount of bottled water, but in its heyday, the numbers were thought to be around several hundred gallons a day. The water in this hotel rivaled any of the other mainstream mineral water sources with the amount of intake. With the smell of mineral water, it's hard to believe that people would drink it, let alone bathe and swim in it. If it would cure you of your ailment though, it was well worth being uncomfortable with the smell and taste.

Even with the success that the hotel had early on, it wasn't able to last forever. Some say that World War II helped lead to the demise of the hotel. I can believe that it helped to some extent because with the war being fought overseas by our parents, children and relatives, it would make it very difficult to go somewhere just to get pampered.   People were so concerned about their loved ones fighting overseas, that I am sure they were doing whatever they could to help the cause stateside. Whether that meant working overtime to create things used in the war or if it meant using your extra money to buy war bonds, the last thing you would do is go to a spa to spend money and relax.   It was around this time that the swimming pools were drained of their water.

By the 1950's and 60's, the hotel was in the midst of some very tough times. By 1971, the Mineral Springs Hotels closed its doors for what they thought would be for good. By the late 70's, it reopened its doors once again to much fanfare. This time it wasn't a hotel that boasted miracle water.   For this reincarnation of the building, it was turned into a shopping mall with various antique and curiosity shops as well as eateries.

With the mineral water running under the building, the river just a block away, limestone deposits all over the area, one would have to assume this building is haunted. All the natural elements can definitely give a building energy, but we need more, don't we?

Many dark tales have made their way out of this building through the years.   Some have truth, some started with truth and then eventually people with creative minds molded the stories, and unfortunately, the building has stories that have been concocted to explain what is going on. Much like I tell the stories on the Alton Hauntings tours, I'll do three of the main stories and let you know what we can prove historically and what may just be tall tales. Please keep in mind that with any story, there are usually several variations of it.   Although the ones I am telling in this story may be a bit off from the ones other story tellers have told, these are definitely stories that have been spread through the area.

The first location I'd like to talk about is the main swimming pool. This story involves a married couple who were going to one of the lavish parties that they used to hold down in the swimming pool area. When you went to one of these galas, you didn't go in your swimming suits. Patrons were expected to be adorned in their finest attire. Women would wear formal gowns and then men would be neck deep into a tuxedo. You would be rubbing elbows with high society at these types of events.

The story goes that they were both getting ready to go to the party when the husband began to grow a little impatient that his wife wasn't ready yet. So far with the story, this is definitely believable am I right guys? The husband decided to go down to the party without her. After being without his wife for some time, the husband was definitely enjoying himself poolside. When the wife finally arrived, she found her no good, two timing man, in the arms of another woman. This enraged the woman so much that she took off her high heel shoe and hit him over the head with it. He fell, bleeding profusely, into the pool and died from his injuries. Now, in his death, he is said to not only haunt the swimming pool, but he also haunts the room they were staying in that night. One of the things people have reported inside the building is a puddle of water that forms outside of one of the rooms. This puddle is attributed to this man, standing, dripping wet, outside the door to their room, trying to get his revenge on his beloved wife. This phenomenon was actually captured on camera during a television show's visit to Alton. Naturally, what they don't show you is the man with a pitcher of water pouring it in front of the door.

Most of the activity I've encountered in the pool area occurred during tours with Troy Taylor. Troy would sometimes bring the entire tour group into the pool and he would stand outside the pool and look down at us. He would then turn out all the lights just to raise the creepy factor to a 9.5. Things were happening frequently enough that putting 45 people into a pool, with one rickety staircase as the only means of escape, was not the safest option. To solve this issue, he reversed the rolls to where only he would go into the pool and all others would look down at him. No matter if you were in or out, there was always a chance that something would go bump in the night.

Several tours, when everyone was standing still in the dark, you could hear hard sole shoes walking around the perimeter of the swimming pool. I can tell you that it gets very dark down there and for someone to do this; you would be risking major injury just to get a scare out of someone. Sure, scaring the tour goers is great, but if you fall face first into the pool, your face would be the main thing scaring people. Not only is there the concern of falling into the pool to worry about, there are also other hazards like debris and concrete columns all around the pool that could cause great harm to a wannabe "scarer".

Crazy Steve had an experience in the pool area during one of the tours. He was standing outside the pool in the dark along with everyone else listening to the stories. When Troy turned on the lantern just to point something out to the crowd, Steve saw a man standing on the other side of the pool. He was wearing a double-breasted suit and was leaning against one of the columns with his arms folded at his chest. Steve watched him the entire time the lantern was on. As soon as the Lantern went out, the room was once again shrouded in darkness and he could no longer see further than what was just in front of him. When Troy finished the stories, and turned the lantern back on so everyone could see their way out, Steve noticed the man was gone. Steve then hustled over to the exit door and looked at each person as they left the room to make sure nobody was wearing a similar outfit. He was not surprised when he found that nobody on the tour fit the description of what he saw.

Other reports coming from the pool area involve voices, shadows, wet footprints appearing and disappearing with no explanation, and various sounds of water movement. Unfortunately, there really isn't any historical documentation that can say what truly happened in the pool. Whether or not the story that explains why this area is haunted is true or not, I can tell you that this is one of the most active locations in the building.

The next location brings us to the bar area of the former hotel. The story here involves a traveling artist who ventured into the river town of Alton and needed a place to stay and to quench his thirst. Along with the talent of painting, this man also had a talent of racking up quite the tab due to his drinking. When he visited Alton, he stayed at the Mineral Springs Hotel and began to indulge in the spirits the bar had to offer. With all the drinking, and no money to pay for it, he struck a deal with the owners and agreed to paint a mural of the city of Alton on one of the walls of the bar. Sadly, prior to finishing the mural, the artist passed away. But death wasn't going to stop this artist from paying off his debt. Employees were shocked to find the mural was mysteriously finishing itself in the weeks that followed the man's untimely death. Not only did the ghost continue to paint the mural, but he has also been seen in the bar area. Generally, when this man is encountered, he is accompanied by a smell of alcohol and smoke. Sometimes a ghostly figure of a man is seen standing with one leg up in the air in this area. Try to not picture a dog relieving himself by lifting its leg up, but rather a man standing at a bar with his foot elevated onto the footrest. You could also think of his pose as a "Captain Morgan" pose.

Creepy story, isn't it? This story sounds great and it also sounds like it's straight out of Hollywood. The issue at hand is there are also no records to back this one up either. There is a mural there, so we do have that. Perhaps there was a traveling artist who painted it as well. The story of him dying and then finishing the mural may have been created to explain the activity that is going on in that area. Sometimes people like to create a story to explain paranormal activity. If there's a back story that can explain what's going on, it makes the ghost story so much more believable and definitely scarier. My thought is this. If there was indeed a traveling artist who painted the mural, I am sure he finished the mural in life and then he probably moved up the river to another hotel or bar and pulled the same stunt by working up a tab and paying for it with his artistic talent.

One of the most popular stories with the hotel involves the main staircase that leads off the main hall. The story here surrounds a couple who had a disagreement in their room one evening while they were staying at the hotel. The argument made its way out of the room, down the hall and stopped at the top of the marble staircase. At this point, the story goes into a couple different directions, but whichever way you go, the outcome is the same. If you turn left on the story, the woman slipped and fell down the stairs, if you turn right, she was pushed. The road comes back to one path at this point because the woman broke her neck during the fall and died right at the bottom of the steps. It was ruled an accident and the man wasn't charged with murder.

This story can actually be confirmed. This really did happen and is the cause to the staircase being haunted. The woman that was pushed down the stairs loved the smell of jasmine and often wore jasmine perfume. Sometimes when she is present on or near the staircase, the smell of jasmine fills the air. Some have reported also seeing a woman actually falling down the stairs. When they rush over to help her, there's never anyone there. Others have reported seeing balls of light on the staircase and some have seen items like signs and curtains mysteriously moving back and forth. Several people have encountered the "Jasmine Lady" all the way up to present time. A previous investigation on the staircase turned up an interesting piece of evidence. During the EVP session, the word "misunderstanding" was recorded. Was this the spirit of the woman who fell down the stairs defending what happened? Maybe the fight was over a misunderstanding, or maybe any accusations of guilt in her accident were a misunderstanding.

There are several other stories with the hotel centered more around the actual rooms. One such story involves the spirit of Pearl, a female resident who committed suicide in one of the upstairs bedrooms. The building is also thought to have a spirit of a little girl as well. She has been seen all throughout the building, but her favorite spot seems to be the pool.

Even though we don't have a lot of tragic stories to explain why some of the spirits linger, the sheer amount of people who entered the doors of that building through its course of operation, have definitely left a mark.

Now, I bring you to the much-awaited, investigation of the building, part of the story. I had been on some adventures there in the past, but only investigated it moderately. Most of the times when I was there it was for a tour and our time is very limited with those. Several members of the Illinois Hauntings Tours were on hand as well as about fifteen investigators during this visit. When we arrived, Troy began giving a detailed history of the building while Dave, co-owner of the "It's Raining Zen" store (located inside the hotel) took Lisa and me around to show some of the locations that have been active. This was great because since he is in the building so much, he could tell us what areas had recently had activity. That's a valuable tool for doing an investigation.

Some of the locations he showed us weren't locations that we knew about. That's often the case with large buildings like this. There's just so much to explore, and we tend to focus on the spots we are familiar with. Sure, the staircase where a woman died would be haunted, and of course the room where Pearl committed suicide would be too, but what about other random spots? He showed us a hallway where people encounter heavy feelings and have heard unearthly sounds. Several rooms in the area of the hotel that they are trying to rehab are active. There's even one room that has some activity occurring that they are think may be caused by former gangsters who stayed at the hotel. In that room, investigators have heard noises and smell cigarette smoke.

The lower level ballroom is also active. It has an area at the end of the large open space that leads to the bathrooms. This area is one of the more active areas in the entire hotel according to Dave. Several people have encountered the spirit of a little girl in this location. Dave even mentioned that some recent investigators captured audio of a child and mother having a conversation in that area. It included something to the extent of the child asking if they could go home and the mom responding with it's not time yet.

He also showed us an area near the swimming pool that a lot of people don't go into. Most avoid it because you have to wind through some passages to get there, and it just seems like it's off limits. There's a metal chair in that room that is thought to be owned by a male spirit named William. William does not like his chair being messed with and usually doesn't care for women being in his area either. My first thought was to somehow convince a girl on the tour to sit in the chair. I, of course, wouldn't tell her why I needed her to sit there either. One of the last locations he took us to was the massive room where they used to bottle the water. This room had a weird vibe to it that's really difficult to explain unless you actively experience it. People have reported seeing a male figure in the far corner of the room wearing a top hat.

With the new knowledge, we made our way up to the main floor and arrived just as Troy was finishing up the introduction. Troy, Lisa and I then gave everyone a tour and showed them all the hot spots and told the stories of what we had just learned. I do want to reference one thing at this point because it'll come back later. When we were up in the room where Pearl took her own life, I noticed a Mountain Dew can sitting on the wall framing just behind me. As everyone gathered in the room, I shined my flashlight just over my shoulder and said "Sometimes a soda can will appear in this room. Let me know if anyone sees one tonight." Of course, this was met with some laughs and a few sneers. Once the tour was complete, we went back to the safe room and everyone went out on their way for the investigation.

Before I get to my adventure, I'll tell you a story that one of my friends had there. He's actually a customer of my store and I was working on this story when he came in. I told him I was writing a story about the overnight we did and he said he investigated there before. I asked if he had any experiences he could share and he did.

Joe and three of his friends took part in an event there back in October of 2015. As the hours passed and it got later and later, there weren't very many people left in the hotel. Throughout the night, they had a couple things happen. Mostly bumps here and there, a couple photos of shadows in the upstairs hallways, even cold spots while down in the pool. They even captured a dark shadow in a photograph taken in one of the rooms upstairs. In the photo, you can see a darker shape to the

**The shadow is located on the right side of the photo.
Photo by Joe M.**

right of the image. This wasn't anything that they were able to see with their own eyes at the time. It was only seen when they reviewed their images later. A similar dark shape was captured on one other photo, but never again on any other of the photos they took that evening.

By four in the morning, they were all tired, and also the only people in their group of four to still be awake! That's when they decided to check out the area behind the pool! This is the same area I mentioned earlier that William is said to haunt. Joe's friend, who I'll call Karen, was with them at the time, which for a man who hates women, probably wasn't a good idea. It didn't hurt that another individual who was with them was provoking the ghost by repeatedly saying "don't you touch her!" Just as well should have told him not to touch the button that says "do not touch", or to set your bankroll on the ground and leave the room with the hopes that someone wouldn't take it.

After a few minutes of provoking the spirit, Joe saw a shadow of a man sitting in the chair about twenty feet in front of them. It was there for a couple minutes, and then all of the sudden the shadow, leaping from the chair explosively, rushed towards the group and Karen was knocked to the ground! She was okay but they got out of there fast, and that was end of the investigation for them! How cool would it be to see someone on your investigative team get physically assaulted by a ghost? I long for the day when I can see Len get molested by a spirit!

After Joe told me this story, I really started questioning a decision I made early on in the investigation. When we started investigating, that room was the first place I wanted to go. During our visit to the room with Dave, I noticed a lot of broken glass lying around the base of several sections of the walls. I love finding vintage bottles and thought it would have been cool to find one of the hotel's mineral water bottles. I went into the room and found it to be rather dark. I only had the flashlight on my phone to aid me, which was just enough to see a little bit in front of me. I then began to search the perimeter for treasures. I didn't totally think things through though by coming down here alone.

As I was in this room, hunkered down searching through the dust and dirt that littered the area where the floor and wall met, there was a whole lot of darkness behind me. My light really didn't offer up much protection. At one point, I even turned around because I heard something and when I shined my light, it was aimed directly at the chair where William usually sits. It was a pretty uncomfortable feeling. What if William was also considered "The Keeper of the Broken Glass," and I was messing with his inventory. I didn't find any intact bottles unfortunately. I am really surprised that I didn't cut my hand open at any point of my search. Regardless if I didn't find any bottles, I did find some other interesting things that made me think a little.

I got up from my crouched position and began walking all around the large room. I found several marbles lying on the ground in various areas of the room. I thought they were cool and wondered if they were old. After about fifteen minutes of looking around, I had about five or six marbles in my pocket. Weighted down by the enormous weight of the marbles, I figured I would head upstairs to go to another area. With pockets sagging, I made my way towards the doorway so I could exit the room. En route to the door, I passed by this tall wooden box that was sitting near one of the support poles, and I noticed a bucket inside of the box. When I shined my light into it, I found a bucket full of these marbles. My heart sunk. Here I thought I found historic artifacts tied to some of the children who came through the hotel's doors and boy was I wrong. What I think I found were noise making props that were possibly used for other purposes during tours and investigations in the building. Throughout the night, I found these marbles all over the pool area and they turned into quite the nuisance when you stepped on one. They definitely could have caused an injury to someone if they stepped on one.

When I do these investigations, I like to set up my camera in one area and just let it run throughout the night. I decided to put it in the swimming pool and have it aimed towards the staircase. This way people would see the red record light as they were coming down the stairs thus nobody should knock it over. I also set it up here because I had a feeling this would be one of the most active areas with investigators, and perhaps they would stir something up for me. After setting it up, I changed focus and made my way up to some of the rooms being renovated. I ran into a few investigators periodically, but nobody was really having anything significant happening yet.

After about 45 minutes, I went back to the pool to grab my camera and move it somewhere else. I decided to set it up in the ballroom for a bit aiming towards the bathroom hallway. There were some investigators in that area already, so if they did any EVP, I could become part of it as well by recording the audio. I stayed in this area for a bit, but then decided to relocate again. I hadn't been down to the bottling plant area yet, so I began my journey down several levels to reach the room. When I got down there, I was kind of hoping that there would be other people in the room, but there wasn't. When I walked into the massive room, all you could see is darkness in front of you. I shined my flashlight, but it wasn't bright enough to see very far in front of me. I even tried to use the infrared on my camera, but my infrared light and extender weren't strong enough either. The room is so massive that the infrared extender doesn't have anything to bounce off of to illuminate the area. So, it really didn't do any good for me.

I was not in there for more than a couple minutes when I started getting a really weird feeling. It was one of those "you shouldn't be in here" kinds of feelings. I started thinking that I could be needed, right at that very second, somewhere else in the building. And for me to be down in that creepy, dark room all by myself was just selfish on my part. My mama raised me to always do good for others and to never put myself first. So, with that, I did the noble thing and backed out of the room very slowly trying very hard not to trip over my own feet. I kept what little light I had in front of me until I got through the doorway and into the hall. Then I moved very hastily towards the stairs and up several flights to the main floor. I found out the sad truth that nobody needed me upstairs, but knowing is half the battle and I needed to be sure.

I then decided to head back down to the pool to see if anyone was investigating in that area. I found the room to be empty, so I was excited to be able to spend some time in there alone. I was going to do a belly flop into the empty pool just for show, but elected to take the stairs since nobody would be there to see the flop. There were several chairs set up in a circle which was evidence that this is an area where people tend to congregate. I picked a random chair, set my digital recorder on a table to record any possible audio, and then just sat still. I find times like these to be a great time to contemplate life. It did not do any good though because I kept coming back to the thought of why I am sitting in an empty haunted pool all by myself.

Early on during this twenty or so minute segment, I did get a little freaked out at one point. As I was sitting there alone in the dark, I saw this ominous shape come through the doorway and then it just stood there looking over the pool. I was gazing up at it trying to figure out who, or what, it possibly was. It just stood there looming, taking the view of the pool in. I dared not breathe, or it may have seen me. At this point I wasn't sure that it was even aware that I was sitting just below it. Thankfully it slowly turned and walked away leaving me to the darkness and my pounding chest.

Not too long after that, I looked towards the shallow end of the pool and saw this white, misty, shape. It was just across from me no more than five feet away, so I figured it must have been one of the chairs. I looked at it for about a minute trying to get my eyes to focus on what it was. I shifted in my chair a bit so I could pull my flashlight out of my pocket and direct it towards the shape I saw. Once I aimed it at the spot where I was seeing the white shape, not only was the shape gone, but there wasn't even a chair in that spot. I am not really sure what it was that I saw. There was nothing there that could have projected the color or the shape that I saw.

The last thing that occurred was at one point I heard what sounded like footsteps moving about. I shined my light towards the sound, but didn't see anyone there. I was hoping that my digital recorder would have picked up the audio. We'll get to that a little later though.

I decided to go back up to the main area and check in with everyone else. Sandy, Kaylan and her two friends were getting ready to head down to the pool, so I came back down with them. I set my video camera up next to the staircase, aiming towards the seating area. We all grabbed seats in the chair circle and set up our various devices. I had my digital recorder running as well as my ghost radar. I believe Sandy was also using a radar and some of the others were using recorders and cameras.

After a little bickering over who was going to start the EVP session, Kaylan stepped up and began asking questions. The rest of just sat there and enjoyed the atmosphere the pool was offering us. Troy ended up coming down after a while and asked the group if I was down there. I answered him and he informed me that he was the one who came down earlier when I was in the pool. He didn't want to say anything because he wasn't sure who was in there and he didn't want to ruin anyone's investigating. I knew the thing I saw had an ominous vibe! He sat with us for a few minutes and then he ran up to the safe room to get a piece of equipment. When he returned, he came back into the pool and started walking toward the shallow end with his new investigating gadget. Then he did his best Japanese horror movie impersonation.

In the center of the shallow end of the pool, unbeknownst to Troy, was a pile of trigger objects people have left in the pool. There were little toys and other items used to garner a response from the pool's inhabitants through the years. Troy, not seeing these, began to step on and smash several of these items. I guess I could say he was like Godzilla or maybe the Incredible Hulk, because Troy Smash. Troyzilla has a ring to it actually and it's not far off from how it looked to all of us.

After startling us to death, he then made his way over to us. The gadget he had was called a Ghost Arc. It's a really cool device that has pretty lights and lots of buttons. It measures all sorts of environmental changes. It even records audio among other things. We played around with it awhile and asked a lot more questions before wrapping the pool visit up. My video camera light was flashing which meant that I had two hours of video in the books. Because of that, I was ready to move on from this spot as well.

By the time we got to the first floor, most of the investigators had already left for the night. It was probably only about 30 mins later that we did the rounds to make sure everyone was gone and the doors that should be closed, were closed. At this point, the only remaining people were Troy, Lisa, Sandy, Kaylan and Me. When we went upstairs to the area that was being rehabbed, I had to take advantage of something I saw earlier that night. When you are going down the hallway, it makes a right hand turn down another hall. Just before that right-hand turn, I noticed a two-foot by two- foot hole cut out of the bottom of the wall. After you turn right down the hallway, you can squeeze through the framing of the walls and get to that hole. So, I ventured up ahead of the others and hid myself behind that hole. Then when the victims, I mean my friends, got up to me, I started reaching at their ankles. I even did the best zombie moan this side of the Mississippi! Although I did catch a couple of them off guard, most of them knew I was up to something because I moved a little too quickly to get ahead of them.

It turns out Kaylan had an experience upstairs in Pearl's room which she showed us while we were shutting the floor down. When she was up there with several other people, the soda can I made reference to earlier flew off the board it was resting on and landed a good three to four feet away. They left the can where it lay and when I looked, I noticed some liquid stains around the can. When I picked it up, it had a lot of soda still in it. So that meant when it was sitting on the board, it had weight to it. It wasn't just an empty can. It was obvious something with force had to of pushed it off the shelf, I don't think just a breeze could have done it. If it was empty, sure, a gust of air from a window, or even someone walking past could have possibly knocked it down. In this case, I am not so sure.

Once we deemed the entire building secure, we gathered our stuff and talked a bit about the investigation. We compared notes and then with how late it was, we all left the building and went our separate ways.

Later, when I got time, I started to review the audio. This is my evidence.

For the digital recorder, when I was down in the pool by myself I did have one thing of note occur. This was after Troy had already come down. This meant he was gone and I was in there by myself once again. On the audio, you can hear the footsteps I mentioned earlier in this story, walking around the swimming pool. You can even hear me turn on my flashlight to aim it at the sound and then you hear about one more step being taken before they quit entirely.

Although I did record a little audio throughout the evening in various places, I came up empty on most of it.

The pool seemed to be the hot spot for EVP's that night. Luckily, I had one more segment to listen to from that area. This was the thirty-minute session I did with Sandy, Kaylan and her friends, as well as a couple others who tagged along. This segment was actually pretty active.

As soon as the audio started recording I picked up several dripping sounds. It's not falling at the same interval as you would think something that was dripping would do. It's kind of sporadic. It was picked up again later during this segment. I find it interesting that at no other point on my recordings in the pool area, did I pick up this sound. I also mentioned it to another group that had been down there for a long time early on in the investigation, and they never once heard that sound. So, I am not really sure what caused it. But hey, we are in a haunted swimming pool, why shouldn't there be dripping water sounds.

Early on in the recording, I also picked up a weird mechanical kind of noise. I am not really sure what it is or what may have caused it. Either way, it was definitely out of place and wasn't similar to any other noise I captured. It kind of reminds me of the sound cassette players make when it is rewinding.

There was one time during this part of the evening where the recorder picked up a really loud bang. When I first heard it, I thought maybe it was the noise we heard when a lady bumped into a couch that was down there. We were all sitting in the pool when this happened and it scared all of us because we weren't expecting it. Sandy even referenced at this point that she may have wet her pants which I informed her that the pool isn't supposed to have water in it, so she had to stop soiling her pants. When I heard this bang on the recorder, I knew it wasn't when the lady made the noise because none of us made reference to the sound. That means this was a different noise that we didn't hear when it actually occurred.

One of my favorite parts of this segment was the sound of a female voice saying "hello". None of us heard this with our own ears or we would have said something when it occurred. It's very clear. It seems to be said within all of us talking as well which seems a little rude since it was an interruption of our conversation. I asked Sandy and Kaylan if they remember hearing someone say hello, but they didn't. Kaylan thought that maybe "hello" came up on a radar and one of the girls down there repeated what it said. This was debunked though because after checking the logs, hello was never said through the device.

There was an additional audio clip when Troy went all ballistic on the items that were lying at the bottom of the pool. When he is done causing a ruckus, (can I describe this ruckus) just as the noise is finished you can hear what sounds like a woman scream. Perhaps this is the same female that said hello. It's hard to say, because it could have been the sound you make when you try not to laugh at something too. So maybe one of the members of our group was trying to keep the laughter in and it came out as a squeaky noise that sounded like a scream.

The only other interesting audio I picked up during this segment was what sounded like someone whispering. I can't figure out exactly what's being said, but it's there and it definitely wasn't us. When I tried to pull it off the recorder, I did my best to clean it up. I temporarily became a top-notch sound engineer and managed to kind of get rid of some of the background noise and bring the voice out a bit. Even then, it's not the best though. Hopefully if you are taking part in the interactive part of the book and listening to the actual

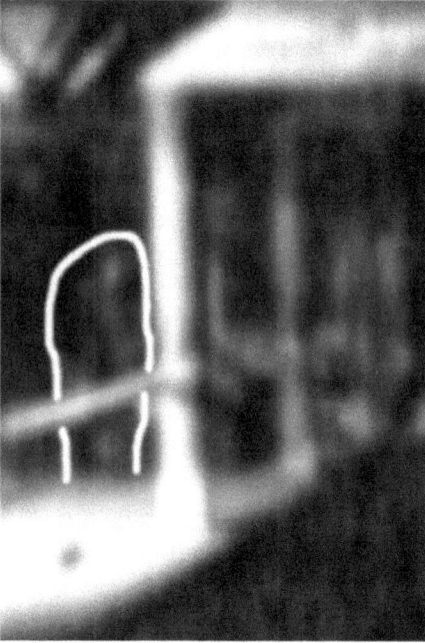

There's a shape of a person inside the white lines. Photo taken by Steve Mangin.

audio files, you'll be able to hear it. It's very faint and is underneath my voice. It sounds like several small words being said.

Aside from the audio, I also took some photos and of course still had the video camera footage to watch. After looking at my photos, I didn't capture anything exciting. Luckily, my good pal Crazy Steve took a lot of photos that night during the investigation. I asked him if he was able to get anything good, and as usual, he did. When Steve takes pictures, it's all about the law of averages. Steve takes a crazy (see what I did there) number of pictures every investigation. It's because of the magnitude of photos he takes that he is often times able to capture something. The Mineral Springs was no different.

When Steve takes a photo, he's using some special settings on his camera. Although I have no idea what these things that I am about to tell you mean, here it is for you to hopefully understand. Steve uses ISO 4200, no a/f illuminator and he also uses no flash which means he gets his only light from ambient sources. The photos come out in a grainy, grayish kind of look. With these settings, he tends to get a lot of shapes that look like people. Sometimes they are black shapes, which could be shadow people.

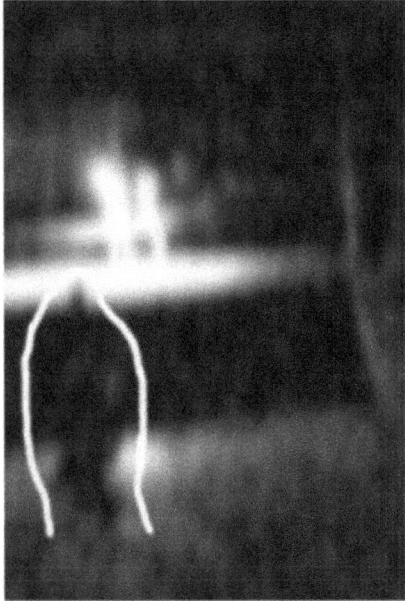

Dark shadowy figure in the shallow end of the swimming pool. Photo by Steve Mangin.

Other times they look like they are human. He submitted several good photos from the investigation of which I selected two that are included in this story. One of the photos has what appears to be a shadow person in the shallow end of the pool. The other image looks like a person standing outside the pool. When both of these photos were taken, there were no individuals near that could have contaminated the evidence.

After reviewing my video recordings, I am reminded about how boring this field can sometimes be. It's so hard to stay focused and watch the video with the hopes that something happens. The video was actually pretty uneventful. Every location I moved it to throughout the evening had a little action, but nothing concrete. One good thing about the video is that I was able to debunk some of the audio I captured. For example, earlier I mentioned I picked up this weird mechanical sound that I compared to a tape recorder. The camera picked up the audio as well which is ideal. The first time that sound happened I noticed on the video that a lady had just turned on her own digital camera. The second time I picked up that noise, that same person turned their camera on again. So, by using multiple tools, it aided me in debunking my findings since I was able to concur that the sound was just her camera turning on.

When I had the video camera running down in the pool with Sandy, Kaylan and others, there was a lot of dust floating around. I know some investigators would be very excited with these white balls of light coming from nowhere, but I am going to go ahead and say it was nothing more than dust and debris. The pool was full of this stuff. When you have the amount of people we had moving throughout the building all evening, they were bound to kick some things up. Plus, we were down there shifting about and moving our feet across the floor which helped the dust move about.

Although I only recorded about two hours of video, I was very hopeful that I would have captured something exciting. The only excitement was the Troyzilla moment I mentioned earlier. Although the camera wasn't aimed at him when he did it, we did get his reaction from the explosion. He said some obscenities about the fact that people left all this "stuff" laying there on the pool floor. It was actually quite entertaining to hear, but I would have loved to of had video proof of the moment as well.

I am hopeful this won't be my only adventure back in the building. I love the building and always have. It was very close to possibly being torn down recently, and I am thrilled to see the new owner reviving this grand hotel. Perhaps these renovations will ignite the paranormal activity there as well. I am sure the resident spirits will be happy with the changes to the building and grateful that they will continue to have a home. If you are in the Alton area, and you haven't been to this location before, please do yourself a favor and visit the building and please enjoy the stores it has to offer. It's the new owner and these shops that keep the history of The Mineral Springs Hotel alive.

CLOSING

I hope you enjoyed the newest book. Each time I do an investigation and document the events, it inspires me to continue doing this. There are times where it's difficult to get the time to track down investigations, and even harder to find the time to do the actual investigation. Whether I have experiences or not, I enjoy the stories and enjoy even more, putting them down on paper for you to read. I am very grateful that you not only purchased the book, but that you also read it. It's very humbling to know that people out there want to know what I have to say.

Hopefully reading this didn't make you feel like you were reading a book. I want you to feel that I am right with you telling the story! We could have been story telling by a campfire, maybe across from each other at a coffee shop, or if you like to read in bed, well, maybe let's just have separate beds like they did on the "*Dick Van Dyke Show*".

I also hope that you took advantage of going to my website www.ghostsneversayboo.com so you could hear some of the audio. I didn't put it all up there because some of it is questionable at best. Still, having the option to listen to some of the evidence is pretty exciting.

I've already got some stories lined up for the next book! So, as I send this off to be edited, which I do feel sorry for the work the editors have ahead of them, I am looking forward to doing some investigations and getting started on the next book!

Until then, here's to the future! If you are a ghost book reader, thanks for going on the adventures with me. If you are an investigator, may I wish that a full-figured apparition chases you down some dark and deserted hallway. If you only read this because you are an "obligated" friend of mine, thank you for helping me feed my children.

Luke Naliborski
Summer 2017